Malibu's Cooking Again 2

CATHY ROGERS

Dear Deborah,

What a special soul you are.

A true treasure

Happy Cooking

Much Love always.

Cathy 3/05/2024

ISBN: 978-1-73462-190-7

Cover Art by Delores Purdy.

Editing by Gina Burrell.

Interior Layout by Rachel Greene for elfinpen designs.

Cover by Amelia Greene.

Photos on pages 21, 97, 107, and 127 by USDA Forest Service, courtesy of Peter Buschmann. Licensed in the public domain.

Photo on page 133 by Dave Hoefler on Unsplash.

A Note from the Author

My earliest memories are memories of food. My grandmother Cecilia making her famous coffee cake…My mother Netta preparing for a dinner party, even though she had been on her feet the whole day preparing food at the country club where she worked. My uncle Jack showing me how to make homemade sausages. My mother-in-law Edie talking to me every morning, when I was first married, about what I was going to make for dinner. …My aunt Rosie letting me cook with her in the kitchen when we visited her in Berkeley…When my beloved mother-in-law Edie passed from this world my new mother-in-law Sue shared her special love of cooking with me…My friends saving me when my daughter died by making me teach them how to cook and insisting they pay me. I was to write up the recipes and they would be at my house next week... Then there was a call from U.C.L.A. Can you teach at our University next semester? … An amazing offer to teach classes on the Silver Sea Cruise Line. Teaching at all the major cooking schools in California and the wonderful students who have attended have enriched every element of my existence. A wave of food has always orchestrated my life. Cooking for my amazing husband, two sons, daughter-in-law, sisters-in-law, brothers-in-law, nieces, nephews and special friends has filled me with gratitude. Preparing food and beautiful recipes has stayed with me through thick and thin, it is my way now of giving back to this world which has been so generous and loving. Teaching others how to prepare food has given me purpose. Thanks to my amazing cousins who have changed my life in such incredibly caring ways, we share this legacy of food.

When the Woolsey Fire burned so many homes of my special friends and neighbors, saving their recipes and adding to them in a beautiful book combining lasting memories and stories, seemed like the best way for me to help Malibu heal. Even when life glues your feet to the ground and you think all is hopeless, cook a wonderful meal and this will lift your spirits. Being able to show others the beauty of preparing food has allowed me to fly higher then I ever thought one person could. Food can be a spiritual journey, it is for me. This book was written for people who have believed that something greater can be accomplished through the efforts of kindness and passion. Malibu's Cooking Again is a tribute to the amazing resilience of the people who live and work in Malibu. They are my hero.

Introduction

What is it like to live in Malibu? There are no words to describe the gratitude. It is an area filled with natural beauty, animals of all kinds, people of every walk of life from the rich and famous to people that are trying to make ends meet every day. People from all over the world come to surf in its oceans, dine in famous restaurants, shop or just want to enjoy the view. Whatever it is you come here for, when you live here, it is your home. There are people who you work with and play with and love. It is a place where you have raised your children and seen so many changes. It is also a place where people come together to pray and to help one another.

Malibu is all that. When one of our neighbors is suffering we all suffer. There are so many heroes in our community that work so unselfishly hard to make everyone's lives better. That is what a community does. It is an extension of a family when sometimes there is not one. People helping one another to make sure no one suffers. From the firemen to the neighbor next door, these extraordinary souls came together when that time was needed. The stories and photos are inspiring.

When I think of healing and making things better, food always comes to mind. Millions of books have been written and photos have been taken about food. There is so much to be said for eating around a table and sharing something delicious. You can face anything knowing that this amazing world has given us the ability to give energy and happiness through our mouths. When we go a little farther and create beauty on a plate the whole experience is even more elevated.

In our second cookbook we want to share some wonderful recipes and stories. Friends whose homes were evacuated. Having their community invite these families and their animals to a safe place where their needs will be met, tells you what you need to know about this unique community. May you always dream and know that when your heart is in your dream, anything can happen. May your journey be one of peace and may you always remember to be kind. It is the true spirit of Malibu.

Acknowledgements

Where does one start to thank the people who are true angels in your life. The people who show up and say, I am there to make this happen. Julie Ellerton is one such person. She is not only an amazing photographer, she is a friend and true spirit of generous, loving kindness. I thank-you Julie for your caring and special gift that truly brought this book to life. The added dividend was Ron Lander who is a genius with a computer. His guidance helped put this book together. Without Rachel Greene, there would not be a Malibu's Cooking Again 2. Rachel's kindness, patience and tremendous skill is what you are seeing on these pages. Thank-you Rachel with all my heart! You are a gemstone. My niece Annie Gingold who came over and with her artists eye and took the photos of each recipe. Sally Robles who first typed every scrape of recipe I had to make it readable. Love you and thanks! Marina Drasnin is an amazing artist and photographer who has a heart of pure gold. The photos with words of wisdom were her gift to Malibu.

To my wonderful Prince Charming husband Jeff, who makes all my dreams come true. He sampled all the recipes and shared his opinion. Because of Covid, he was the soul taste tester of this book.

My dear friend Gina Burrell who worked on the first cookbook for Malibu. She is a truly gifted cook and rallied her friends who sent in stories and recipes that I cried reading. This world is one beautiful ball and Malibu is blessed with the best there is. She came over and worked on my personal computer to make sure every recipe was perfect. You are amazing Gina.

Dolores Purdy, artist extraordinaire, took Julie Ellerton's idea of a whale sprouting hearts from a photo Julie took in Malibu. Dolores expanded on this idea and created this truly remarkable work of art that is our cover. Her idea is the story of the Malibu survivors. So many people have the deeds to their home but insurance sometimes not always covering all the cost of rebuilding. She designed the cover to be a deed that would manifest into the whale's dream of blowing hearts of love to the residents with prayers that they would be able to rebuild soon. For this cover, she used an original deed from 1863. The grey whale is not colorful in real life, he is here! This truly talented artist brought tears to my eyes. When I began working on this book, we stayed at an incredible resort in Utah, The Amangiri Resort. Diana Allen was one of the first people who welcomed us at the front. She asked where we were from and we got to talking and I said I was working on a cookbook for the people who lost their homes in the Woolsey Fire. I was looking for an artist to do the cover. She said to look at the work of an artist I carry in my gallery shop. It was Dolores Purdy. I had no idea what she would create and if she would do this at all. What a wonderful idea and gift we received with this cover.

Lauren Lobley, who helped in so many ways even with being in the eighth month of pregnancy, with her second child. She did not stop trying to help and showed such dedication. She gave us a wonderful gluten free pancake that is truly delicious. You can read her story with it.

Karen and Arnold York continue to bring a community together everyday with the Malibu Times. They are treasures and gifts to everyone making sure Malibu is up to date always. They should be honored every moment. Shivani who wrote about the cookbook in the Malibu Times to rally support and to ask for recipes from the community, thank-you.

There will always be a special place for Marlene Alder Marks who, in 1993, helped write the first Malibu's Cooking Again. You will be remembered with love always.

There are two people that I could not have been more blessed to have in my life. Teresa Morales is an angel and truly remarkable person. She taught me so much. Gracias.

Suri Fuentes always has a smile on her face. She is positive and sees the bright side in all situations. She is a beautiful soul. Gracias.

To my wonderful husband who sampled and tasted all the recipes and shared his opinions. He also shared some of the history of Malibu by loaning his collections that were photographed with certain plates. I am beyond blessed to share my life with this incredible human being. Together with our two sons Ryan and Chad, who grew up in Malibu, this community truly holds my heart. Our dog, Desi, walks everyday and knows exactly where all the dog treats are in the shopping centers.

Marina Drasin provided all of the beautiful inspirational graphics used throughout the book. Marina is a Los Angeles photographer/painter with her work in collections worldwide. She studied at the Sorbonne University in Paris and received a B.A. at the School of the Museum of Fine Arts/Tufts University in Boston. The daughter of two architects, Marina learned early on that a creative lens on the world is a gift to be shared, and the magic of the everyday moment a gift to be celebrated. This recent body of work captures this magic as it lives and breathes through modern urban existence, from Los Angeles to Paris. Find out more about her work at marinadrasnin.com.

Lastly to all the people who make Malibu beautiful. There are many, from our shoe man, to our cleaners, post offices, urgent care clinics, restaurants, schools, churches, synagogue, groceries and stores which we go to everyday. We could not survive without you. Let's hope Malibu will grow and prosper forever!

Finally, Malibu Cooking Again 2 was made possible through the efforts and assistance of the following Steering Committee and people with great talents and vision. Sincere thanks and gratitude for all you have done. Sometimes when I cut into a fruit or vegetable I see a heart. I think in the very core of this earth is the most beautiful heart. This universe is so filled with love. We are all connected by this love. It nourishes us and gives us the opportunity to help make this world one. Whatever gift you are given, use it. Help the world be filled with the brightest light, you.

Cathy Rogers, Chair
Jeff Rogers
Annie Gingold
Julie Ellerton
Gina Burrell
Beverly Hammond, Image Maker Publishing Co.
Dolores Purdy, Artist
Dianne Allen, Amangiri
Lauren Lobley

Ron Lander
Marca Kaufer, Benefactor
Helene Eisenberg
Karen and Arnold York
Vicky Pearson
Linda Conrad Feldhorn
Sally Robles
Marina Drasnin

With much humbleness and thanks,
Cathy

Contents

Food feeds our souls.
Love enables us to
care for one another.

Appetizers

Avocado, Bacon and Tomato Cones

Serves 6 | Prep Time 60 | Cook Time 20

WHY I LOVE THIS RECIPE: A really unique, tasty and unusual snack! This wonderful recipe is like having a bacon, lettuce and tomato ice cream cone. How much fun for everyone to enjoy. The batter can be made ahead of time and frozen. Thaw overnight in the refrigerator and use what you need. Refreeze remaining batter for another use. If you decide to bake the cones, they will stay fresh in a tightly covered Tupperware or a plastic bag for a week. Note. Instead of baking on parchment paper, you can purchase a plastic liner called a silpat at kitchen stores.

INGREDIENTS YOU'LL NEED

Cone:
1/3 cup softened butter
½ cup plus 2 tablespoons powdered sugar
¾ cups flour
2 egg whites
¼ cup chopped chives or cilantro
* * *
2/3 cup Homemade Mayonnaise (see Sauces, Stocks, and Vinaigrettes)
* * *
4 slices smoked bacon
* * *
1 ripe avocado
1 red tomato, peeled, seeded, and diced
1 yellow tomato, peeled, seeded and diced
Sea salt to taste
Pepper to taste
6 small leaves butter lettuce
Lemon

DIRECTIONS

The batter for the Cone will make 1½ cups batter more than you will need for this recipe. You can freeze the remainder for another time. For Cones, cream the butter and powdered sugar together. Incorporate flour a little at a time. Add the egg whites and mix just until thoroughly mixed. Chill overnight in refrigerator, then bring to room temperature before spreading.

Cut round 4" circle from cardboard paper. Place on parchment-lined or silpat lined cookie sheet. Spread 1 tablespoon batter thinly over circle. Sprinkle with chives or cilantro. Remove circle and bake 400 degrees 4 to 5 minutes or until golden brown. Remove from cookie sheet and place tightly around cone shape. A carrot with a pointed tip works as a good cone shape if you cannot find a wooden dowel. Let stand briefly. Remove to pipe stand.

Cook bacon and make sure it is crispy. Remove to plate and reserve. Reserve one piece of bacon for garnish. Break up bacon into small pieces. Cut avocado into very small dice. Season tomatoes with salt and pepper; mix in lettuce, bacon, and Homemade Mayonnaise. Set aside.

Mix avocado with salt and lemon juice. Fill each cone with bacon mixture, then with an ice cream scoop up avocado and place on top. Sprinkle with reserved 1 piece bacon. Serve and enjoy!

Braised Beef in a Cone with Avocado

Serves 8 to 12 | Prep Time | Cook Time

WHY I LOVE THIS RECIPE: The Barbecue Sauce that is needed in this recipe (can be found in Chapter 7), it makes 4 1/2 cups, but this recipe calls for 3/4 cup. The Barbecue Sauce will last 6 months in the refrigerator. The cones are so delicious , you can fill them with anything. They are even great baked flat if you do not feel like rolling to a cone. just enjoy!

INGREDIENTS YOU'LL NEED

Browned Beef with Stock: May be made ahead of time and frozen
5 short ribs
Sea salt to taste
1 teaspoon Dry mustard
¼ teaspoon Paprika
Dash Pepper
1 onion, chopped
3 carrots, chopped
3 celery stalks, chopped
5 whole garlic cloves
5 stalks thyme
1/3 cup extra virgin olive oil
* * *

Cone:
1/4 cup sugar
1 1/2 tablespoons sweet butter
1 tablespoon honey
1 1/2 tablespoons heavy cream
1/2 teaspoon vanilla extract
1 tablespoon flour
* * *

Filling for cones:
2 tablespoons olive oil
1 onion, chopped
2 green onions finely chopped
1/3 cup red pepper finely chopped
2 braised short ribs, cooked
3 garlic cloves, minced
Sea salt to taste
¾ cup Barbecue sauce (see Sauces, Stocks, and Vinaigrettes)
1 teaspoon chili sauce with garlic
* * *

Avocado Topping:
1 ripe avocado
Sea salt to taste
Juice from 1 lemon wedge
1 shallot, chopped
1 teaspoon green jalapeno, diced

DIRECTIONS

For Meat, season short ribs with salt, mustard, paprika, and pepper. Heat pan and sauté meat until brown on both sides. Brown the vegetables and place in pan with meat. Deglaze pan with water and pour over meat.

Cover pan and bake at 475 degrees for 2 hours. Reduce heat to 200 degrees and bake 4 hours more. Cool in pan.

Strain broth. Remove fat from broth and meat. Freeze broth and meat separately. May be prepared in advance and frozen

For Filling for cones, heat olive oil in skillet and cook onion until golden brown. Add red pepper and saute until lightly golden. Add green onions and garlic. Sauté a few moments more.

Chop short ribs. Add to onions and season with salt, Barbecue sauce, and chili sauce. Cook 30 minutes. Set aside.

For cones, In a small saucepan combine the butter, sugar, honey and the cream. Bring the mixture to a boil stirring with a wooden spoon. Boil for 5 minutes. Remove from heat and stir in vanilla and flour. Dot by large teaspoons onto a silat lined cookie sheet. Bake in a 400 degree oven for 5 minutes or until golden. Remove. Cool slightly and wrap around a cone or carrot to make a cone shape. Cool. They harden quickly. You can place in the oven for a few seconds to soften and roll, if they get hard. Enjoy!

For Avocado topping, combine all ingredients.

Place short ribs into cone and top with scoop of avocado topping. Serve and enjoy!

Caramelized Phyllo with Red Onion Confit

Serves 6 | Prep Time | Cook Time

WHY I LOVE THIS RECIPE: The sweet crisp of the phyllo cracker, the bite of the wasabi caviar, the savory delight of the onion confit is memorable. This is a sure winner and a very unique recipe. Make your own mayonnaise well in advance. It will last weeks in the refrigerator. That is if you don't use it before. The caramelized phyllo stay fresh in the freezer once made. They are then ready to use whenever you need them.

INGREDIENTS YOU'LL NEED

1 tablespoon Homemade Mayonnaise (see Sauces, Stocks, and Vinaigrettes)

* * *

Chili Vinaigrette (see Sauces, Stocks, and Vinaigrettes)

* * *

Homemade Mayonnaise (see Sauces, Stocks, and Vinaigrettes)

* * *

3 phyllo slices
¼ cup canola oil
1/3 cup sugar

* * *

¼ cup olive oil
½ large red onion, thinly sliced
Sea salt to taste

* * *

6 tablespoons homemade mayonnaise
6 tablespoon Crème Fraiche – can be purchased in the market
1 teaspoon horseradish
3 ounces Wasabi caviar - can be purchased at a restaurant supply house or at an Asian market.

* * *

2 tablespoons minced chives

DIRECTIONS

Preheat oven to 425 degrees. Cut each phyllo sheet in half. You should have 6 sheets. Spread each phyllo sheet on board and brush generously with canola oil. Dust with sugar. Stack one sheet on top of the other. Brush with remaining canola oil and sugar. Keep repeating this process until all six sheets of phyllo are used. Cut phyllo into 1-inch squares. Carefully place squares on parchment-lined cookie sheet. Cover phyllo squares with another sheet of parchment paper and top with a cookie sheet that is weighed down with a brick, to prevent from curling up. Bake for 10 minutes or until golden brown. Lift brick to check if golden brown. If so, remove cookie sheet and parchment paper. Turn phyllo over and bake 5 minutes more. Set aside.

Sauté onion in olive oil until caramelized and golden brown. Season with sea salt. Reserve. May be made earlier in the day or the day before. Mix together Homemade Mayonnaise, Crème Fraiche and horseradish. Place one caramelized square on plate and top with a little horseradish cream. Layer, starting with another phyllo square, then onions and caviar. Top with 3rd remaining phyllo square. Dot plate with Chili Vinaigrette and herb leaf. Repeat to make desired amount. Serve and enjoy!

WATTA POP 1¢

Chicken Mousse Lollipops with Cotton Candy

Serves 8 to 10 servings | Prep Time 15 minutes | Cook Time 20 minutes

WHY I LOVE THIS RECIPE: Who does not like cotton candy. There is a twist to this cotton candy however. Packed into the center is a heavenly bite of chicken liver mousse. This little recipe is so easy to prepare. The best part is that the chicken liver mousse freezes well and you can use as much as you want and save for another time. If you like instead, you can place the balls of mousse on the lollipop stick and freeze. Then you have as many as you like for another time and all you have to do is start up your cotton candy machine. I purchased a small one on line. They are reasonable and work very well. If you change the color of your sugar crystals, you change the color of the cotton candy.

INGREDIENTS YOU'LL NEED

CHICKEN LIVER MOUSSE
4 ounces chicken liver
1 tablespoon cognac
⅔ cup heavy cream
3 tablespoons sweet unsalted butter
½ teaspoon Himalayan salt
2 egg yolks
* * *
COTTON CANDY
2 tablespoons sugar crystals
Lollipop sticks

DIRECTIONS

Make the mousse. Heat oven to 300 degrees. Line a small 4" by 2 ½ " loaf pan with plastic wrap. Let edges of plastic go over sides of pan. Puree liver with cognac, cream, butter, salt and yolks in a food processor until very smooth. Strain through a fine strainer into a bowl, Pour into prepared lined loaf pan. Fold the excess plastic over the top of pan.

Place loaf pan into a larger baking dish and fill halfway with boiling water. Bake until firm. Check after 20 minutes. Chill overnight. Roll into small ball and place on the lollipop stick.

Heat a cotton candy machine and when the cotton candy is ready, gently wrap mousse with the cotton candy. Repeat with as many as you need. Chicken mousse maybe frozen for another time.

Enjoy.

Hamachi with White Peaches, Avocado, Baby Spinach and Sake Glaze

Serves 4 to 6 | Prep Time 15 minutes | Cook Time no cooking required

WHY I LOVE THIS RECIPE: I always keep ahi tuna and hamachi in my freezer at all times. It is perfect for a quick lunch or light dinner. I have used peaches and avocado in the recipe, but any fruit or vegetables can be substituted. Always make plenty of homemade mayonnaise and sake sesame sauce in the refrigerator too. Enjoy!

INGREDIENTS YOU'LL NEED

1/2 pound hamachi tuna, sushi grade

2 ripe peaches or nectarines peeled just before serving

1 avocado- using a small melon baller, cut balls out of avocado

20 to 30 baby spinach leaves

red beet glaze (see Sauces, Stocks, and Vinaigrettes)

sake sesame sauce (see Sauces, Stocks, and Vinaigrettes)

dill oil

1/2 cup homemade mayonnaise (see Sauces, Stocks, and Vinaigrettes)

1 tablespoon wasabi powder or freshly grated wasabi

DIRECTIONS

Slice hamachi about 1/8 inch thick. Mix mayonnaise with wasabi and generously brush on each plate. Space hamachi over mayonnaise spacing by 1 inch. Slice peaches and place between hamachi. Place avocado in between peaches and hamachi. Place spinach leaves standing up in between hamachi. Dot with beet glaze and sake sesame sauce. Season with Pink Himalayan salt. Enjoy.

Short Ribs with Onion Ring Volcano

Serves 6 to 8

Why I love this recipe: These short ribs are so tender and so decadent that even just the smell will make your taste buds go into a frenzy. Serve them with mashed potatoes or any vegetable of your choice and let the meat do the rest of the talking. There will be an eruption of happiness from you family and guests when they eat this. If your bar-be-que sauce gets to thick, dilute with a little chicken broth.

INGREDIENTS YOU'LL NEED

6 to 8 short ribs
sea salt
dry mustard
Hungarian paprika
freshly ground pepper
2 tablespoons extra virgin olive oil
3 carrots chopped
1 red onion chopped
3 sacks celery chopped
6 garlic cloves
3 thyme sprigs
1 teaspoon peppercorns
water to cover
1 cup red wine

Onion Rings:
2 cups canola oil
1/2 cup flour plus 1 tablespoon
1 teaspoon baking soda
1/2 baking powder
dash cayenne
2/3 cups cold soda water
1 or 2 red onions, chilled 1/2 -inch thick, carefully separate
into rings. You will need 3 per person
1 cup Barbecue Sauce – See Sauces section for recipe

DIRECTIONS

Season short ribs with sea salt, dry mustard, Hungarian paprika and freshly ground pepper. Heat olive oil in a roasting pan. Add short ribs and brown very well on all sides. Brown vegetables in a pan until very golden. Add vegetables to the meat. Deglaze the pan that you browned the vegetables in, with wine and water. Pour liquid over short ribs. Cover with liquid. Bring to a boil and cover. Bake for 1 hour in 425 degree oven. Reduce heat to 375 degrees and bake 2 hours more. Reduce heat to 225 and bake 6 hours. Let cool in oven. Strain broth to use for stock. Chill stock and then remove fat. Short ribs maybe frozen or kept in the refrigerator. Remove back fat while warm. Season with a little extra sea salt before heating and serve with Barbecue Sauce. Chill shorts ribs and cut in one inch pieces. Stick a lollipop stick in center. Heat in oven 350 degrees for 20 minutes. For onion rings, heat oil to 375 degrees. Place 1/2 cup flour in bowl. Add baking soda, baking powder and cayenne. Stir in soda and make a creamy mixture. Dip one onion ring in flour and then batter. Place in hot oil and cook until golden. Drain on Paper towels and continue with remaining onion rings. Serve and enjoy! Place hot short rib on plate and top with three onion rings on each plate, larger on bottom and smaller on top. Place barbecue sauce around. Enjoy!

Hamachi with Truffle, Truffle Caviar and Crispy Onions

Serves 6

WHY I LOVE THIS RECIPE: This is a wonderful recipe to add to your sushi resume. It is so easy to make. most everything can be made ahead. The wasabi mayonnaise and the sake glaze for sure. The only last minute is frying the shallots. Once you taste this recipe, you will make it again and again. "On Friday , August 30th, I walked out of my house to take my dog Desi for a walk. I looked into the sky . Did I see smoke coming from that mountain. OMG! This cannot be happening again. Stay calm and take deep breaths . All around me , I saw people taking photos. I was praying not again!"

INGREDIENTS YOU'LL NEED

1/2 pound fresh hamachi
2 tablespoons white truffle oil
Truffle salt
1/3 cup wasabi mayonnaise (see Sauces, Stocks, and Vinaigrettes)
1/3 cup sake glaze (see Sauces, Stocks, and Vinaigrettes)
2 brown mushrooms julienned
1 tablespoon white truffle oil
1 garlic clove minced

CRISPY SHALLOTS
6 shallots sliced very thin
1 teaspoon dry mustard
1/2 teaspoon smoked paprika
2 tablespoons flour
Himalayan salt to taste
1 cup organic canola oil

1 tablespoon truffle honey or1/2 teaspoon truffle oil mixed into honey and dash truffle salt
1 tablespoon truffle caviar

DIRECTIONS

Freeze hamachi for 3 hours or more. When ready to serve, heat oil in a small sauce pan to 375 degrees. Mix shallots with dry mustard, paprika, and flour. Mix to coat well. Drop in hot oil and fry until golden brown. Place on paper towels to drain. Season with salt.

Remove hamachi from the freezer and thaw slightly. Heat a small sauce pan and add a little truffle oil. Add mushrooms and saute until lightly golden. Reserve. Slice hamachi 1/8 inch thick with a sharp knife. With a brush place a little wasabi mayonnaise on each plate. Place hamachi over. Place a few sauted mushrooms on hamachi. Season with truffle salt and drizzle a little truffle oil and honey over. Top with 1//8 teaspoon optional truffle caviar. Top with fried shallots and enjoy.

Japanese Kobe Sliders in Chinese Bao with Brie, Fig Jam and Caramelized Onions

Serves 6 to 8 | Prep Time | Cook Time

WHY I LOVE THIS RECIPE: Eating these little heavenly baby Kobe burgers on the perfectly soft Chinese bun is an experience in itself. Enjoy.

INGREDIENTS YOU'LL NEED

Chinese Bao – makes 24 buns, freeze the remaining:
1 tablespoon dry yeast
1 teaspoon sugar
¼ cup flour
¼ cup warm water
* * *
½ cup warm water
1½ cups all purpose flour
¼ teaspoon sea salt
2 tablespoons sugar
1 tablespoon canola oil
½ teaspoon baking powder
* * *
Caramelized Onions:
1 small onion
1/3 cup olive oil
1 teaspoon balsamic vinegar
1 teaspoon Agave nectar
Sea salt to taste
* * *
Hamburgers:
½ pound Kobe ground beef
Sea salt to taste
Freshly ground pepper to taste
* * *
6 to 8 slices brie
2 tablespoons fig jam
* * *
2 tablespoons Homemade Mayonnaise, spiced with wasabi if desired (see Sauces, Stocks, and Vinaigrettes)

DIRECTIONS

For Homemade mayonnaise, heat olive oil in small skillet over low heat. Add shallots and sauté until translucent. Add garlic and cook 1 minute. Remove from heat and cool. Set aside. To make wasabi mayonnaise, just add some wasabi paste to your mayonnaise.

Place either egg yolk or egg white in work bowl of food processor. Add the reserved sautéed shallot/garlic mixture and remaining ingredients, except oil. With motor running, slowly add canola oil. If mayonnaise gets too thick, add water and lemon juice. Place in container and refrigerate until ready to use.

For Chinese Bao, mix together yeast, 1 teaspoon sugar,1/4 cup flour, and ¼ cup warm water. Let stand 30 minutes. Mix in ½ cup water, 1½ cups flour, ¼ teaspoon salt, 2 tablespoons sugar, and 1 tablespoon canola oil. Knead until dough surface is smooth and elastic. Roll over in a greased bowl and let stand until triple in size, about 2½ to 3 hours.

Punch down dough and spread out on floured board. Sprinkle baking powder evenly on surface and knead for 5 minutes. Divide dough into 2 parts and place the piece you are not working on in a covered bowl. Divide each half into 12 parts. Shape each part into a ball and place face down on a wax paper square. Let stand covered until it doubles about 30 minutes. Repeat with second half. Bring water to boil in wok and reduce heat to medium. The water should be slightly boiling. Place plate on rack. Place buns on plate; cover and steam 15 to 30 minutes. Cook remaining buns and set aside. Cut 6 to 8 buns in half.

For Caramelized Onions, heat olive oil in medium skillet. Sauté onions 20 to 30 minutes under low heat until lightly golden brown. Stir in balsamic vinegar and agave nectar. Season with sea salt. Set aside.

For Hamburgers, shape meat into 6 to 8 baby burgers. Season with sea salt and pepper. Heat grill and brush buns with butter. Cook burgers until charred. Brush buns with mayonnaise and caramelized onions. Place a hamburger on a bun, over the onions. Top with brie and fig jam. Place other half of bun on top and serve. Enjoy!

Mozzarella Marinara

Serves 4 to 6 | Prep Time Requires preparation ahead of time too firm. Cooking time, 20 minutes | Cook Time 15 minutes

WHY I LOVE THIS RECIPE: Can you imagine what the sensation of fresh melted fried cheese, that has been kissed by a delicious marinara sauce? Wow! It does not get better. You can even coat the cheese with the breading and freeze. You can even make the marinara sauce and freeze. It will make your life so organized by planning ahead for unexpected company. Vine-ripened or heirloom tomatoes are the best. Always shop organic!

INGREDIENTS YOU'LL NEED

4 to 6 2 oz. pieces of mozzarella cheese (not the soft or fresh, it's in a large ball - cold
¼ cup flour
1 egg, beaten
½ cup fresh breadcrumbs - can also use Panko breadcrumbs
* * *
Marinara Sauce (see Sauces, Stocks, and Vinaigrettes)
* * *
2 cups canola oil
4 to 6 fresh basil leaves

DIRECTIONS

Cheese may be sliced in any size and shape you want. For an appetizer, you may cut into small triangles. Dip each piece of mozzarella first in flour, then in egg, then in bread crumbs. Refrigerate on a plate lined with plastic wrap. Refrigerate 2 to 3 hours.

Heat canola oil in fry pan to 375 degrees. Fry basil leaves, one at a time, for about 30 seconds. Keeping oil hot, fry cheese until golden on all sides.

Heat Marina Sauce. Place a little Sauce on plate and top with fried mozzarella and one fried basil leaf. Serve and enjoy!

Portobello and Shiitake Mushroom over Pesto with Puff Pastry Crust

Serves 6 | Prep Time 40 minutes | Cook Time 35 minutes

WHY I LOVE THIS RECIPE: This recipe reminds me of a French pizza. You have all the workings of a delicious pizza without the dough. Instead, you use flaky and delicious puff pastry. I love making my own. If you prefer, many bakeries and markets sell it frozen. It is just delicious. Any vegetable may be substituted for the mushrooms. Sliced blanched yellow and green zucchini is great. Just remember whatever vegetable you use cook it first and dry it well or saute it. The excess water in the vegetables will cause the crust to be not as crisp. By placing a small salad on top, it gives you a beautiful and well-balanced meal. Enjoy!

INGREDIENTS YOU'LL NEED

3 tablespoons sweet butter
5 tablespoons olive oil
3 large Portobello mushrooms, thinly sliced
Sea salt
Freshly ground pepper
3 large Shiitake mushrooms, thinly sliced
* * *
Pesto:
2 fresh garlic cloves
½ cup pine nuts
2 cups Fresh basil leaves
1 teaspoon sea salt
½ cup olive oil
1½ cups fresh grated Parmesan cheese
* * *
1/2 pound Puff Pastry or Detrempe: - may be made in advance and frozen
Detrempe:
½ pound bread flour
½ pound all-purpose unbleached flour
3 ounces sweet butter, chilled and cut into 6 pieces
Pinch salt
1 cup ice water

1¼ pounds sweet butter, chilled
¼ cup unbleached flour
* * *
1/2 cup Red Wine Vinaigrette – may be made in advance and refrigerated:
¼ cup red wine vinegar
¼ cup water
1 tablespoon sugar
1 teaspoon dry mustard
1 tablespoon Dijon mustard
1 teaspoon Worcestershire sauce
2 garlic cloves
¾ cup canola oil
¼ cup olive oil
* * *
3 cups Boston lettuce, julienne

DIRECTIONS

Heat 1/2 amount butter and olive oil and sauté portabello mushrooms until lightly golden brown. Reserve. Season with sea salt and pepper. Heat remaining butter and olive oil in pan, sauté shitake mushrooms until lightly golden brown. Reserve. Season with sea salt and pepper.

For Pesto, in work bowl of food processor, finely chop garlic and pine nuts. Add basil leaves and process until all ingredients are pureed. Add salt and olive oil until very green. Stir in Parmesan cheese. Store in container in refrigerator until ready to use. Serve at room temperature.

For Puff Pastry, or the Detrempe, place all ingredients, except the iced water, into work bowl of food processor. Process until the butter and flour are thoroughly combined. With machine running slowly pour ice water through the feed tube. Remove dough and wrap tightly and refrigerate about 30 minutes. Place a large plastic board in freezer. Place rolling pin in freezer, too.

Place the ¼ pound of butter in bowl. Sprinkle with flour and knead with your hand until flour is incorporated with butter. Place in a 6" x 9" rectangle dish and wrap in plastic. Refrigerate until firm.

Remove the Detrempe from refrigerator. Cut a deep cross in the dough. Spread out the sections of the dough so that the center is the thickest part. Roll the dough out from each section to form a four leaf clover. Try to keep the center a little thicker. Place the butter in the center and bring the edges of the Detrempe to the center. It is like enclosing the butter in an envelope. Cover pastry with plastic wrap or tin foil. Chill 1 hour.

Remove pastry from the refrigerator, and roll into a large rectangle, cutting into 6 squares and trim edges. Brush each square with Pesto and layer mushrooms, alternating portabello mushrooms and shitake mushrooms. Chill 1 hour. Bake 375 degrees for 15 to 20 minutes or until bottom crust is brown. Bake on parchment lined cookie sheet.

For Red Wine Vinaigrette, combine all ingredients, except oils, in work bowl of food processor. With motor running, slowly add oils through feed tube. Pour into squeeze bottle and refrigerate until ready to use.

Toss julienne lettuce with 3 tablespoons Red Wine Vinaigrette. Save the rest of the Vinaigrette in the refrigerator for future use.

Place a little lettuce on top of the Puff Pastry. Place on plates. Serve and enjoy!

Red Pepper Crepes with Lobster, Onions and Dill Vinaigrette

Serves 6 | Prep Time | Cook Time

WHY I LOVE THIS RECIPE: Crepes are everyone's favorite. By adding some roasted red pepper to the crepe batter, you have changed the color and added a slightly different taste. The lobster filling with the dill brush makes a perfect marriage. These small crepes are a different first course or starter. They are also delicious for brunch.

INGREDIENTS YOU'LL NEED

Red Pepper Crepes:
1 red pepper, peeled, seeded, roasted
1 egg
½ cup flour
2 teaspoons sugar
½ cup milk
1 tablespoon oil
Dash salt
* * *
1 cooked lobster, meat removed and diced
¼ cup diced chives
½ cup diced red onion
⅓ cup remoulade dressing
1 teaspoon sweet relish
Juice of ½ lemon
Sea salt to taste
* * *
Dill Vinaigrette (see Sauces, Stocks, and Vinaigrettes)
Beet Glaze (see Sauces, Stocks, and Vinaigrettes)

DIRECTIONS

To make Red Pepper Crepes, place roasted pepper and egg in work bowl of food processor. Add remaining ingredients and process until smooth. Let stand 30 minutes and strain. Heat a non - stick 8" sauté pan over medium high heat. Add 1 ½ tablespoon batter and tilt pan. Cook until edges are golden, about 40 seconds to 1 minute. Cook about 10 seconds on other side. Continue with remaining batter. Stack between plastic wrap. Makes about 12 to 14 small 3 inch crepes. Reserve.

When crepes are finished, mix lobster with chives, red onion, remoulade, sweet relish, lemon and sea salt, Spread on each crepe. Roll up crepes tightly like a jelly roll. Wrap in plastic wrap and refrigerate.

Prepare Dill Vinaigrette and set aside. Any leftover dressing can be stored in refrigerator for several weeks and used for other salads.

When ready to serve, brush plate with 2 tablespoons dill vinaigrette and place two crepes on side. Dot with beet glaze. Serve and enjoy!

Tuna Parfait on Tempura Japanese Sweet Potatoes

Serves 6 to 8 | Prep Time 10 minutes | Cook Time 10 minutes

WHY I LOVE THIS RECIPE: A pillow of sweet potato in between the crunch of a wonderful tempura. This alone would be enough. When you top this with a tuna parfait, you have gone over the top! Make sure to always freeze raw fish for 30 minutes to an hour before slicing. This is to make sure to kill any foreign bacteria that could be in the fish. **Make sure to buy your fish from a reputable fish monger and that the fish is very fresh. Try to use Japanese sweet potato if you can. It is white inside with a red skin, and the texture is perfect for the tempura. I like to cook the potatoes ahead and refrigerate, then just peel and slice and dip into the batter and fry until golden. What a delicious treat.

INGREDIENTS YOU'LL NEED

Tuna Parfait:

1/3 pound fresh Ahi tuna (Sushi quality), minced

¼ teaspoon sea salt

½ teaspoon agave

½ teaspoon ginger, grated

1 shallot, peeled and minced

1½ tablespoons cilantro, minced

½ tablespoon lime juice

1 teaspoon jalapeno chili, minced

½ teaspoon sesame oil

¼ teaspoon mushroom soy sauce

1 tablespoon Homemade Mayonnaise – (see Sauces, Stocks, and Vinaigrettes)

* * *

1 small white Japanese sweet potato, baked

1 green onion, cut in half and then cut horizontally

* * *

Tempura Batter:

Dash cayenne pepper

1 cup cold club soda

¼ cup all-purpose flour

½ cup rice flour

1½ cups canola oil

* * *

Sake Soy Glaze

1/3 cup tamari

1/4 cup rice wine vinegar

2 garlic cloves crushed

1 tablespoon grated onion

1/2 teaspoon grated ginger

1 tablespoon cane sugar

1 tablespoon sesame oil

1/2 tablespoon sake

Mix all ingredients together and refrigerate until needed

DIRECTIONS

Prepare Homemade Mayonnaise for the Tuna Parfait and set aside.

For the Tuna Parfait, in a small bowl, combine all ingredients, except the mayonnaise. Add Homemade Mayonnaise; set aside.

Heat 1½ cups canola oil in a small frying pan to 375 degrees. Remove peel from sweet potato and cut into rectangles 3 inches x ½ inch, or any size you like.

For the Tempura Batter, mix rice flour with cayenne pepper. Whisk in cold club soda. Dip potatoes into flour, then Tempura Batter. Fry until golden.

Repeat the same process with the green onion. Season with sea salt and drain on paper towels.

Place potato on small plate. Top Tuna Parfait on each potato. Garnish with green onions.

Prepare Sake Soy Glaze and set aside.

When ready to serve, dot the glaze on plates for garnish. Enjoy!

Tostones with Salmon Tartare by Gina Burrell

Serves 4 to 6 servings | Prep Time 15 minutes | Cook Time 15 minutes

WHY I LOVE THIS RECIPE: "Plantains once fried are great just by themselves. You can add a little caviar or creme fraiche too." This is a great appetizer when people come over. It is also a great lunch dish or first course. The salmon maybe substituted with tuna if you desire. Special thanks to Peter Selman for the gorgeous photo.

INGREDIENTS YOU'LL NEED

PLANTAINS
4 ripe plantains
Canola oil
Sea salt

TOSTONES
1 1/2 pound sushi grade salmon-skinless-into 1/4 inch dice
2 tablespoons dijion mustard
1 tablespoons chipotle juice from can or less depending on taste
1/4 cup drained capers
1/4 cup finely chopped scallions
3 tablespoons olive oil, extra virgin is best
3 tablespoons chopped cilantro
sea salt and pepper

AVOCADO CHIPOTLE RELISH
3 ripe haas avocados- peeled and diced
1 tablespoon pureed chipotle peppers, or to taste
2 tablespoons fresh lime juice
3 tablespoons creme fraiche

DIRECTIONS

For tostones, heat oil to 325 degrees. Slice plantains 1/4 inch thick. Add plantain slices to oil and fry until soft. Drain on paper towels. Heat oil to 375. Flatten slices with the palms of your hand, between two pieces of Saran Wrap, not making them to thin, about the size of a silver dollar and re-fry until crisp. Turn them over in the oil. Drain on paper towels and sprinkle with sea salt to taste.

For Salmon Tartare, Combine all ingredients and season to taste. Reserve.

For Avocado Chipotle Relish, place avocados, chipotle and lime juice in a bowl and mash until smooth. Add creme fraiche and fold until almost smooth. Season.

Take Tostones, place salmon tartare on top and top with avocado chipotle relish. Garnish with cilantro leaves. Enjoy.

PAIRS WELL WITH: Champagne, tequila and beer

Ahi Tuna wrapped around Flaxseed Cracker with Wasabi Caviar

Serves 6

INGREDIENTS YOU'LL NEED

6 , 2 ounce slices of sushi quality ahi tuna
6 Flaxseed Crackers (see recipe for Warm Spinach Salad with Flax Crackers)
3 tablespoons wasabi caviar
3 tablespoons wasabi mayonnaise
1/2 tablespoon plain yogurt
1 tablespoon mayonnaise
Himalayan Salt to taste

6 quail eggs
1 teaspoon sweet butter

DIRECTIONS

Place each slice of tuna on piece of saran wrap and cover with another piece of saran. Gently pound thin. Remove top piece of saran. Place 1/2 teaspoon wasabi mayonnaise in center of tuna. Place cracker over. Wrap tuna around cracker using saran. Remove saran and place on plate. Heat butter in non-stick pan and remove quail egg from shell and cook sunny side up in pan. Season with a dash Himalayan salt. Garnish with dots of wasabi caviar. Mix yogurt with mayonnaise and brush on plate. Garnish with cooked quail egg and enjoy.

Fresh Strawberry Jello Log with Dragon Fruit, Dates and Lace Crisps

Serves 6

INGREDIENTS YOU'LL NEED

Strawberry Jello:
1/4 cup cold water
1 tablespoon gelatin
1/4 cup boiling hot water
2 pints fresh strawberries or frozen thawed
1/3 cup sugar

Fruit and Crisps:
1 ripe dragon fruit peeled and sliced.
2 dates chopped coarsely,
18 blueberries
6 mint leaves
Lace cookie Crisps (see recipe for Short Rips with Onion Ring Volcano)

DIRECTIONS

Pour the cold water in a small pyrex bowl and sprinkle gelatin all over. Place gelatin in a pot of hot water and place on stove. Allow gelatin too liquify. Puree strawberries with sugar in food processor. Strain into a medium bowl to remove seeds. Heat 1 cup of the strawberry mixture and add to when gelatin is liquified . Pour remaining strawberry mixture into gelatin and stir well. Line a 8 by 8 inch pan with Saran Wrap and pour strawberry mixture in. Chill overnight. Cut into 6. Strips and remove saran and place on plate

Garnish with fruit , mint and cookie crisps. Dot with strawberry puree. Enjoy.

The ocean and everything in it holds a gift

Soups, Salads and Vegetables

Yellow Beet, Red Beet, Yukon Gold, Red Potato and Spinach Chips

Serves 4 to 6 servings | Prep Time 10 minutes | Cook Time 30 minutes

WHY I LOVE THIS RECIPE: "A crunchy treat with grilled fish, meat or chicken. Just right on their own they are perfect!" I love making colorful recipes that make you smile when you see them. Eating them becomes even more pleasurable. We always eat with our eyes first.

INGREDIENTS YOU'LL NEED

2 yellow beets, peeled and sliced very thin
2 red beets, peeled and sliced very thin
1 Yukon potato, sliced very thin
1 red potato, sliced very thin
20 baby spinach leaves
2/3 cup organic canola oil
Himalayan sea salt

DIRECTIONS

Heat canola oil to 275 degrees. in a 12 inch skillet. First fry Yukon and red potatoes until all water is released but not brown. Drain on paper towels twice. Reserve on parchment paper. Fry yellow beets to same way as potatoes. Reserve. Fry red beets and reserve. Make sure to drain on paper towel. Reserve on parchment paper.

When ready to serve, heat oil to 375 degrees and fry all vegetables until crispy but not browned. Enjoy. Season with Himalayan Salt. I stacked these through a needle on a bagel holder. They can just be tossed with the spinach leaves for color. Enjoy

PAIRS WELL WITH: Chardonny or Champagne or Beer

Warm Spinach Salad with Flax Crackers

Serves 6 servings | Prep Time 30 minutes | Cook Time overnight dehydration for crackers

WHY I LOVE THIS RECIPE: "The combination of warm spinach on a crispy flax seed cracker is out of this world. The quail egg adds an extra taste treat." This is a great dish for vegetarians. Just leave off the quail egg. It is wonderful to make extra rye flax crackers. They last a long time and are a wonderful snack. Enjoc

INGREDIENTS YOU'LL NEED

Spinach Salad

4 cups fresh spinach leaves, chopped finely 2 shallots finely chopped

1 garlic clove minced

2 tablespoons extra virgin olive oil 3 tablespoons red wine vinegar

1 tablespoon honey sea salt to taste

2 teaspoons Worcestershire sauce

Flax Rye Crackers

1/2 cup dark flax seeds 1/4 cup ground flax seeds 1 tablespoon honey

1/4 tablespoons extra virgin olive oil

1 1/2 tablespoons ground caraway seeds 1/2 cup water

Quail eggs 6 quail eggs

1 tablespoon white vinegar

DIRECTIONS

For spinach salad, combine spinach in a bowl with one chopped shallot. For dressing, heat olive oil and saute remaining shallot until golden brown, add garlic and saute a few moments. Add honey to pan with red wine vinegar, Worcestershire and salt. Bring to a simmer and cook a few moments. Just before serving pour over spinach and toss.

Place on plate. Garnish with flax crackers and poached quail egg.

For flax crackers, combine all ingredients in a bowl and stir in water to make a smooth paste. Spread out thinly on silpats. Cut into cracker shapes with a pizza cutter. Place in 175 degree oven overnight or until crispy.

To poach quail egg, cut with a serrated knife and drop in simmering water which 1 tablespoon vinegar has been added too. Cook 1 minute and reserve. To reheat, place in hot water and garnish

Brie and Prosciutto Filled Chile Rellenos on a Bed of Figs and Arugula

Serves 6 | Prep Time 60 | Cook Time 20

WHY I LOVE THIS RECIPE: The word "brie" alone should have already been enough to capture your attention! But can you even imagine how amazing that melty goodness must taste mixed with prosciutto dripping out of a perfectly executed chile relleno? The mixture of saltiness and spices and sweetness from the figs is exactly what your mouth is constantly craving. This dish gets all of those flavors in one bite and leaves you spooning the rest of the brie off the plate with the lick of a finger.

INGREDIENTS YOU'LL NEED

Pesto - may be made in advance and refrigerated: 2 fresh garlic cloves
1/2 cup pine nuts
2 cups Fresh basil leaves
1 teaspoon sea salt
1/2 cup olive oil
1 1/2 cups fresh grated Parmesan cheese
* * *
3 slices Prosciutto, julienne and chopped
1/2 cup Brie cheese, chopped
1 cup Jack cheese
3 Anaheim chiles, roasted, seeded, peeled, cut down the middle without cutting all the way through.
* * *
6 egg whites
Sea salt to taste
2 cups canola oil
6 tablespoons flour
* * *
Caramel Pine Nuts - can be made in advance and stored in a plastic bag in the refrigerator:
1/4 cup sugar
1/3 cup pine nuts
* * *
2 tablespoons Red Wine Vinaigrette (see Sauces, Stocks, and Vinaigrettes)
* * *
1/2 cup Garlic Cream Reduction:
2 cups heavy cream
10 garlic cloves, minced
* * *
1 1/2 cups arugula
1/3 cup figs, diced

DIRECTIONS

Mix together prosciutto, brie, and jack cheese. Season with freshly ground pepper. Stuff inside of chili with a little pesto and cheese mixture.

Beat egg whites with a little sea salt until almost stiff. Heat canola oil to 375 degrees. Beat in flour a little at a time. Place a little batter on plate. Place cheese stuffed chilies on plate; top with more batter to enclose. Carefully slide chili into hot oil. Brown on both sides. Place on paper towels to drain. Continue with remaining chilies.

For Caramel Pine Nuts, heat non-stick 7" skillet over high heat until hot. Add sugar and let it melt. Add pine nuts and place on parchment paper. Cool.

For Garlic Cream Reduction, combine cream and garlic gloves in small saucepan and simmer until liquid is reduced to 1/2 cup.

Mix arugula, figs, and Caramel Pine Nuts together. Season with a little Red Wine Vinaigrette. Divide arugula on plate. Top with chilies, Pesto, and Garlic Cream. Serve and enjoy!

Burrata with Beet Glazes, Balsamic Reduction, and Dill Oil

Serves 8 as appetizers | Prep Time 15 minutes | Cook Time 10 minutes

WHY I LOVE THIS RECIPE: I love this recipe because it will bring to artist out in you! It is so easy to prepare and is so delicious. The wonderful taste of burrata with these delicious glazes is over the top! Enjoy

INGREDIENTS YOU'LL NEED

1 large ball burrata cheese
2 red beets
2 yellow beets
1/2 cup balsamic vinegar
3 tablespoons raw honey

Dill Oil
1 bunch dill
1 bunch chives
1/2 cup organic canola oil

DIRECTIONS

Cut burrata into 8 pieces. Place large sheets of plastic wrap on counter. Place 1 piece of burrata in center of plastic and wrap tightly. Refrigerate. Prepare vinaigrettes.

For beet glaze, clean beets and cut off top and bottom. Save leaves and cook like spinach. So delicious and filled with good vitamins. Place red beets into a microwave bowl and fill halfway with water. Cover with a plate and cook on high in microwave for 8 to 12 minutes or until tender. Cool in bowl. Peel skin off by rubbing with a paper towel. Reserve beets for another occasion. Add 1 tablespoon of raw honey to the liquid and reduce to 2 tablespoons or until lightly thick. Continue with yellow beets.

For balsamic glaze, place balsamic vinegar in a small pan and add 1 tablespoon honey. Reduce until lightly thick. Reserve.

For dill oil, remove hard stems from dill. Discard stems and hard pieces. Bring a pan of water to a boil, drop dill and chives in water and cook 1 minute. Remove herbs and place ice over to stop cooking. Place herbs and canola oil in blender and blend until pureed and green. Place in a large measuring cup, cover and refrigerate. Strain out herbs the next day. Use right away or freeze.

When ready to serve, make designs with the beet glazes , dill and balsamic. Carefully unwrap each burrata and carefully place in the middle of the plate. Season cheese with sea salt and pepper

PAIRS WELL WITH: Peach Champagne

Caesar Salad in Parmesan Cones with Shredded Parmesan and Sauted Quail Eggs

Serves 6 to 8 | Prep Time | Cook Time

WHY I LOVE THIS RECIPE: This is an example of how much fun you can have playing with food ideas. The only rule in cooking is to have fun.I like to mix my food up as I cook. I never sacrifice taste or eye appeal however. This will change cooking to a true art experience.

INGREDIENTS YOU'LL NEED

Cones - may be prepared in the morning and filled just before serving:

12 to 16 tablespoons grated fine Parmesan cheese

* * *

Caesar Dressing:

1 egg yolk

1 tablespoon Dijon mustard

1 teaspoon English dry mustard

1½ tablespoons agave

3 garlic cloves, minced

1/4 cup anchovies

1 teaspoon Worcestershire sauce

Dash cayenne

1 tablespoon lemon juice

1/3 cup olive oil

1/3 cup canola oil

* * *

3 to 4 leaves Romaine lettuce

½ to 1 tablespoon sweet butter

6 to 8 fresh quail eggs, removed from shells

3 to 4 tablespoons grated Parmesan cheese, grated with a fine cheese grater

DIRECTIONS

Place a silpat liner on cookie sheet. Make 2 cones by sprinkling 2 tablespoons Parmesan cheese for each cone. Bake in preheated 400 degrees oven for 5 to 8 minutes or until lightly golden brown. Remove from oven and while still warm, roll around cone form or a carrot. Reserve on pipe rack.

For Caesar Dressing, combine all ingredients, except oils, in work bowl of food processor. With motor running, gradually pour in oils. Place in refrigerator until ready to use.

When ready to serve, shred lettuce and toss with Caesar Dressing to coat and bind together. Heat butter in nonstick pan. Add quail eggs. Cook until egg whites are set. Place a little salad inside each parmesan cone and then top with a cooked quail egg and some shredded parmesan cheese. Serve and enjoy!

Corn Pudding

Serves 4 to 6 | Prep Time 20 minutes | Cook Time 45 minutes

WHY I LOVE THIS RECIPE: This is my husband favorite recipe. He loves the texture and flavor of the corn. It is so simple and all natural . When corn is at its peak it is a perfect time to make this recipe. If the corn is not at the sweetest , you can add just a little honey. It is heavenly served with grilled chicken or steak!

INGREDIENTS YOU'LL NEED

4 ears fresh corn, grated
Sea salt to taste

DIRECTIONS

Preheat oven to 425 degrees. Mix grated corn and sea salt.

Place in ovenproof container. Bake 20 to 45 minutes, depending on size of container. Corn mixture should be very brown, but not burned. Serve and enjoy!

PAIRS WELL WITH: Pinot Grigio or Sauvignon Blanc

Eggplant Tempura with Lemon Sauce

Serves 6 to 8 | Prep Time 25 minutes | Cook Time 10 minutes

WHY I LOVE THIS RECIPE: Any cooked vegetable will work perfect with this batter. It is so versatile. The creamy lemon sauce is also a nice touch of flavor. These simply delicate vegetables get elevated to star quality in this recipe. Vegetables are so beautiful and they make you feel so good. They add beautiful color, flavor and so many vitamins to your meal. I believe we should use fresh wonderful food to bring health and vitality to our bodies instead of medicine. Our eye first sees the food and then we get to enjoy it with our taste buds !

INGREDIENTS YOU'LL NEED

1 eggplant, peeled and cubed

* * *

Tempura Batter:
1 cup rice flour
Dash kosher salt
½ teaspoon paprika
1½ cups very cold Club soda
2 cups Canola oil

* * *

Flour for dipping

* * *

Creamy Lemon Sauce – (see Sauces, Stocks, and Vinaigrettes)

* * *

Lemon
Radicchio leaves, asparagus or spinach leaves

DIRECTIONS

For Tempura Batter, combine rice flour, salt, and paprika; gradually add club soda, whisking continuously. Heat canola to 375 degrees in a 10 inch skillet with 2 inch sides.

Dip each piece of eggplant in flour, then in batter. One at a time, place in hot oil and drain. Season with salt. Place in Lemon Sauce while still hot. Season and squeeze a little lemon on top. Place on radicchio leaves and place asparagus on the bottom or side of dish. Serve and enjoy!

PAIRS WELL WITH: Merlot or sake

Yellow or Red Tomato Rectangles. Avocado Balls. Asparagus. Onion Rings in a Horseradish Vinaigrette

Serves 6 servings | Prep Time 30 minutes | Cook Time 10 minutes

WHY I LOVE THIS RECIPE: This is a great presentation meal. Look for beautiful yellow or red heirloom tomatoes. Recipe can also be made with green heirloom if the yellow are hard to find. The smoked salmon and dressing can be made ahead. The avocado balls can be made ahead and wrapped in saran until ready to use in the refrigerator. The asparagus can be blanched ahead and cut. All ready to assemble when your guests arrive. Enjoy!

INGREDIENTS YOU'LL NEED

3 to 4 firm but ripe heirloom yellow or red tomatoes
2 firm but ripe Haas avocados
Himalayan sea salt
6 to 8 cooked and peeled asparagus spears or fried spinach
6 thin slices of smoked salmon, cut in 5 small pieces each.
Lemon juice
⅓ cup baby heirloom tomatoes

ONION RINGS
1 red onion sliced ¼ inch thick
½ cup rice flour
⅔ cups cold club soda
Paprika
Pink Himalayan sea salt
2 cups non gmo canola oil

HORSERADISH VINAIGRETTE
1 garlic clove minced
1 shallot minced
1 tablespoon maple syrup
1 teaspoon Pink Himalayan sea salt
¼ cup red wine vinegar
1 teaspoon prepared horseradish
½ cup extra-virgin olive oil

DIRECTIONS

Prepare horseradish vinaigrette. Combine all ingredients in a jar and shake well. Refrigerate until needed.

When ready to serve remove peel from the tomatoes and slice them about ½ inch thick. Line tomato rectangles on plate and top with avocado balls , asparagus, baby tomatoes and onion rings. Pour a little vinaigrette over and serve. Enjoy

PAIRS WELL WITH: Pinot Grigio or Sauvignon Blanc

Indian Turmeric Pancakes with Salad and Chicken

Serves 6 to 8 | Prep Time | Cook Time

WHY I LOVE THIS RECIPE: This is one of my favorite things to eat. In fact I have it every morning when I am at home. I just omit the salad and sautéed onions. I actually roll it and wrap it in a nori with a little avocado. It fills me up and has great anti-oxidants. This is great for your immune system and is an inflammatory as well.. I use some wasabi , garlic and Tamari for a dipping treat.

INGREDIENTS YOU'LL NEED

Ghee: melt one stick of butter. Let cool. Remove the white foam and the remaining clear yellow butter is the ghee.

* * *

Pancake:

1½ to 1¾ cups liquid egg whites

2 teaspoons fresh turmeric, grated, or 2 teaspoons dry turmeric

1 cup chopped baby spinach minced

½ onion, sautéed in ghee or olive oil until golden

3 tablespoons ghee or olive oil for pancake – see above

Sea salt to taste

* * *

Salad:

1½ to 2 cups fine Napa cabbage, shredded

¼ cup yellow carrots, cooked

¼ cup red carrots, cooked

½ cup chicken, cooked and diced

* * *

Salad Dressing:

1/3 cup homemade mayonnaise – (see Sauces, Stocks, and Vinaigrettes)

Dressings

1 tablespoon greek yogurt

1 teaspoon raw honey

¼ teaspoon red pepper

1 tablespoon lemon juice

DIRECTIONS

For Pancake, heat ghee or love oil in 9-inch non-stick sauté pan. Mix egg whites with turmeric and garlic. Cook in pan and sprinkle over sautéed onions and chopped spinach. Cover and cook until firm. Cut a few moments and slice into cutting board. Cut into small triangles with a pizza cutter. Keep warm.

For Salad, mix all ingredients in bowl.

For Dressing, mix all ingredients in another bowl. Add dressing to salad.

Place pancake on plate. Place salad in center of pancake. Serve and enjoy!

PAIRS WELL WITH: Iced Chai Tea

Maple and Port Candied Sweet Potato with Marshmallows

Serves 6 | Prep Time 35 minutes | Cook Time 2 hours for cooing sweet potatoes. Overnight for the Marshmallows

WHY I LOVE THIS RECIPE: Once you have made the marshmallows, they will last for a long time at room temperature. they can even be frozen . They will be a hit over these delicious sweet potatoes. Follow the directions for baking the potatoes. Even though in this recipe you peel the skin off, this method caramelizes the potatoes. I make these often. Thanksgiving is an ideal time for this recipe. Have fun!

INGREDIENTS YOU'LL NEED

3 large sweet potatoes
½ cup Port wine
½ cup maple syrup
½ teaspoon cinnamon
Sea salt to taste
3 tablespoons sweet butter
* * *
Marshmallows:
¾ cup water
1½ packages powdered gelatin
* * *
1 cup baker's sugar
½ cup agave nectar, divided in half
¼ teaspoon vanilla extract
½ cup confectioners sugar
* * *
Confectioners sugar for dusting

DIRECTIONS

Wash sweet potatoes and wrap in parchment paper and then tinfoil. Bake sweet potatoes in 425 degree oven , about 1½ hours. Reduce oven temperature to 220 degrees and bake 1 hour more or until soft. Remove skin, cool and slice 2" thick. Mix port, maple syrup, and cinnamon. Season sliced sweet potatoes with sea salt. Place sliced sweet potatoes in baking dish and cover with port mixture. Dot with butter and bake at 350o for 20 minutes. Set aside.

For Marshmallows, place 6 tablespoons water in a small mixing bowl. Sprinkle the gelatin evenly over water and let mixture stand 5 minutes. Place bowl over a medium saucepan of simmering water and allow gelatin to dissolve without stirring. Remove bowl from heat.

Meanwhile, combine the remaining water, sugar, and ¼ cup agave nectar. Cook over high heat until it reaches 235 degrees on a candy thermometer. Remove from heat. Pour in remaining agave nectar and place gelatin in mixing bowl.

Slowly add hot sugar to gelatin and beat for 15 minutes on high speed. Beat in vanilla. Spread mixture into a 5" x 8" pan lined with a silpat. Cover pan with plastic wrap and refrigerate overnight.

Line another silpat with confectioner's sugar. Carefully turn marshmallows onto non-stick sheet. Pat with confectioner's sugar and cut into desired shapes.

Dust 6" x 12" glass dish with Confectioners sugar. Pour marshmallow in mixture into pan. Dust top with confectioner's sugar. Wet hands and smooth out.

Dust with more confectioner's sugar. Let stand overnight, covered so that it dries out. Cut with hot cookie cutter. Dust with more sugar. Place marshmallows over Candied sweet potatoes and place under broiler until browned! You can blow torch the marshmallows too. Serve and enjoy!

PAIRS WELL WITH: Chardonny or Champagne

Marlene Mattows Vegetable Casserole

Serves 6 to 8 servings | Prep Time 15 minutes | Cook Time 35 minutes

WHY I LOVE THIS RECIPE: The cheese is this dish can be omitted for vegetarians. It is a great dish that can be prepared in advance and just heated before serving.

INGREDIENTS YOU'LL NEED

1 small cauliflower
3 broccoli stems, peeled
4 large carrots, 1 yellow, 1 orange, 1 white 1 red, peeled
1 1/2 cups brussels sprouts
1 bunch asparagus, peeled
1 yellow squash, sliced
1 green zucchini squash, sliced

3 tablespoons olive oil
1 red onion chopped
1 small orange pepper sliced
1 red pepper sliced
1 yellow pepper. sliced
1 julienne portobello or trumpet mushroom
3 garlic cloves crushed

1/4 to 1/2 pound jack cheese grated. Your favorite cheese maybe substituted.

2 cups brown or white rice cooked
sea salt to taste or truffle salt
Freshly ground white pepper

DIRECTIONS

Cook all vegetables until soft but still vibrant in color. Refrigerate to keep color until ready to serve. Cut all vegetables into 1 inch pieces. Reserve.

Heat olive oil in a medium skillet. Add onion and sauce until lightly golden brown. Add peppers and sauce until lightly brown. Add mushrooms and sauce until lightly browned. Stir in garlic and cook for 1 minute. Season with sea salt or truffle salt and a little pepper. Toss cooled vegetables and cheese.

When ready to serve, Season rice with sea salt and pepper to taste. Divide rice into oven proof bowls or large baking pan. divide vegetables and cheese over rice. bake until cheese is melted and all ingredients are heated through. Enjoy!

PAIRS WELL WITH: Chardonny

Meringue with Mixed Vegetables

Serves 8 to 10 servings | Prep Time 20 minutes | Cook Time 2 TO 3 HOURS BAKING MERINGUE

WHY I LOVE THIS RECIPE: This is a show stopper for sure. It captures the rebirth of spring and the promise of renewal. The colors of the vegetables will brighten everyones spirit. Once they taste this delicious salad, they will feel a beautiful sense of bliss. This is what Malibu is all about.

INGREDIENTS YOU'LL NEED

Meringue
2 egg whites
1/2 cup super fine sugar
dash cream of tartar
1 teaspoon vanilla

Vegetables
1/2 cup purple cauliflower cooked
1 yellow carrot cooked
1 orange carrot cooked
1 red carrot cooked
1 hard boiled egg, separated yolks form whites, chopped
10 sugar snap peas, blanched
20 baby spinach leaves

Thousand Island Dressing
1 egg yolk
1/2 teaspoon dry English mustard
2 teaspoons dijion mustard
1/2 teaspoon sea salt
1 tablespoon honey or cane sugar
1 tablespoon catsup
1//4 cups red wine vinegar
1/2 c up organic canola oil

DIRECTIONS

For meringue, preheat oven to 200 degrees. Place egg whites in the bowl of electric mixer. Add a little cream of tartar and beat on high until soft peaks form. Gradually add sugar and beat until very thick. Beat in vanilla. Line a cookie sheet with parchment paper. Place in a meringue in a piping bag and pipe out 1 inch by 4 inch rectangles , not too thick. Place in oven and bake for 2 to 3 hours or until dry. Cool and carefully remove from parchment by gently sliding a knife under and it will lift right off. Reserve.

Cut vegetables into small pieces and reserve.

When ready to serve, brush some dressing on the top of each meringue and top with vegetables, egg whites, egg yolks and spinach.

Brush side of plates with more dressing. Place one meringue on the side. Serve and enjoy.

Passover Spinach Pie

Serves 8 to 10 servings | Prep Time 20 minutes | Cook Time 35 to 45 minutes

WHY I LOVE THIS RECIPE: Emily Lodmer wrote this, "I am so touched that you are again coming to the recipe rescue, for those of us who have lost everything in the Woolsey Fire.--just as you did for the folks in Eastern Malibu in 1993. Bless you! Somehow in the flurry to evacuate, it did not occur to me to take my recipes. Of course, the thought soon dawned that all my wonderful Ottolenghi, Ina Garten, vegan recipe collection (gift books) --and especially old family recipes were now nothing but ash."

INGREDIENTS YOU'LL NEED

6 tablespoons extra virgin olive oil
4 cups fresh baby spinach, cleaned
2 cups fresh scallions ,about 12
1 cup matzoh meal
1 cup fresh dill
8 large organic eggs
4b tablespoons lemon juice
1 tablespoon honey
2 whole matzoh
Sea Salt and freshly ground pepper

DIRECTIONS

Preheat the oven to 350 degrees. With 1 tablespoon of the oil , grease the bottom and sides of a shallow 2-quart baking dish. Set aside. Chop the spinach coarsely. Heat the remaining oil in a skillet. Add the scallions, and after a few minutes the spinach. Stir until wilted and well combined with the oil. Stir in the matzoh meal and combine well, using a wooden spoon. Add the dill. Remove the pan from the heat. Beat the eggs with the lemon juice and honey until frothy, 4 to 5 minutes. Add the spinach, salt and pepper to taste. Soak the matzohs briefly in warm water un til softened. Mold into the bottom and sides of pan.. Pour the spinach mixture over the matzohs in the pan. Bake 35 to 45 minutes or until the top is nicely browned. Enjoy.

Scrumptious Baked Eggplant by Ellen Francisco

Serves 6 to 8 servings | Prep Time 20 minutes | Cook Time 40 minutes

WHY I LOVE THIS RECIPE: Ellen says, "This is so delicious, cheesy and easy to make baked eggplant dish with an Italian flair. This is one of my favorite recipes and anytime I have served it to guests, they ask for the recipe."

INGREDIENTS YOU'LL NEED

1 unpeeled regular eggplant, sliced into 1/2 - inch rounds
4 tablespoons olive oil, or as needed
1 tablespoon garlic powder or 3 fresh cloves of garlic crushed
1 small onion, chopped
3 cloves garlic, chopped
2 small tomatoes, chopped
1 (10 oz.) package fresh spinach leaves (I sometimes use a bit more)
1/2 cup ricotta cheese
3/4 cup Shredded Mozzarella cheese, divided
3/4 cup Parmesan cheese, divided
1 cup tomato pasta sauce (see Sauces, Stocks, and Vinaigrettes)
2 teaspoons Italian seasoning

DIRECTIONS

Preheat the oven to 350 degrees F. Brush eggplant slices with olive oil on both sides and place them on a baking sheet. Sprinkle the garlic powder over the top. Bake for 10 minutes.

Heat 2 tablespoons of olive in a large skillet over medium heat. Add the onion, garlic, tomatoes and spinach. Cook and stir for a few minutes until fragrant, and the tomatoes have released their juices. Set aside.

In a medium bowl, mix together 1/2 cup of ricotta cheese, 1//2 cup mozzarella cheese and 1/2 cup of Parmesan cheese. set aside.
Place the eggplant slices in a greased 9 by 1q3 inch baking dish. Top with the spinach mixture. spoon the cheese mixture over the spinach , and spread to a thin layer. Sprinkle with the remaining mozzarella and Parmesan cheese over the top . Sprinkle with the Italian seasoning.

Bake for 30 minutes in a preheated oven, or until heated through and the eggplant is easily pierced with a fork. Serve with chicken, fish or meat or by itself with a salad or vegetable. It is also good the next day-reheated.

PAIRS WELL WITH: pinot grigio or Sauvignon Blanc

Snap Peas. Fava Beans. Carrots. Heirloom Tomatoes in a Chile Garlic Sauce with Mustard Vinaigrette

Serves 6 to 8 | Prep Time 10 minutes | Cook Time 15 minutes

WHY I LOVE THIS RECIPE: "Vegetables were purchased at the Thorne Family Farm Stand and my favorite, Pacific Coast Greens. Gina Burrell's sons helped harvest at the farm, and sold corn and flowers when they were in high school to Malibu residents." This is another example of the beauty of fresh vegetables. I always buy organic and love to frequent the local farmers markets wherever I am. You simply cannot get better quality. In this recipe, I have used a Japanese chili sauce to flavor the vegetables. If you do not like spice, you can by all means omit the chili sauce with garlic and just it a soy-sesame flavor. The mustard vinaigrette also brings in a delicious surprise taste. The combination of both sauces is a great marriage. This will delight family and friends.

INGREDIENTS YOU'LL NEED

Garlic and Chili Oil
1/4 teaspoon chili sauce with garlic
½ cup Japanese rice wine vinegar
¼ cup tamari
¼ cup raw honey
1 cup canola oil
2 teaspoons sesame oil
* * *
Vegetables:
¼ cup olive oil
36 baby onions, peeled
5 garlic cloves crushed
½ cup Sake
2 cups Chicken Stock or water (see Sauces, Stocks, and Vinaigarettes)
Mustard Vinaigrette (see Sauces, Stocks, and Vinaigrettes)
2 cups fresh fava beans, blanched
6 to 8 blanched brussels sprouts
36 fresh sugar snap peas, blanched
36 baby carrots, blanched
2 small yellow beets cooked and peeled
2 small candy cane beets cooks and peeled.
Sea salt to taste
36 small yellow teardrop tomatoes
10 leaves, baby spinach leaves.

DIRECTIONS

For Vegetables, heat olive oil over medium high heat. Add pearl onions and sauté until golden brown add garlic and sauce a few minutes. Add Sake and reduce to a glaze. Add reserved Chicken Stock or water and simmer 20 minutes. Remove onions and reserve. Boil stock and reduce to about ¾ cup. Bring stock to boil and add onions, Fava beans, sugar peas, and carrots and cook a few minutes. Season with sea salt. Mix in ½ cup Garlic and Chili Oil. Place on plate and garnish with tomatoes baby spinach and Mustard Vinaigrette. Serve and enjoy!

PAIRS WELL WITH: Malbec

Onion Soup with Lamb Lollipops in a Demi Glaze

Serves 6 to 8 servings | Prep Time 15 minutes | Cook Time 10 t0 15 minutes

WHY I LOVE THIS RECIPE: Fantastic Recipe! The lollipops can be frozen and cooked last moment. The soup and the glaze can both be prepared and frozen as well. This makes entertaining so much easier. Have the best time.

INGREDIENTS YOU'LL NEED

½ lamb tenderloin cut into 6 to 8 inch pieces
Sea salt
Freshly ground pepper
6 to 8, 3 inch pieces smoked bacon
* * *

ONION SOUP
1 small maui or sweet white onion, chopped
¼ cup extra virgin olive oil
1 cup chicken broth
⅓ cup heavy cream
2 Tablespoons sweet butter
Sea salt
Freshly ground white pepper
* * *

Garlic Glaze
½ cup reduced beef broth
⅓ cup port or Madiera wine
3 minced garlic cloves
Dash of salt
2 tablespoons sweet butter

DIRECTIONS

Season the lamb tenderloin with sea salt and pepper. Freeze. Heat olive oil in pan over high heat and grill frozen lamb pieces until very brown on each side. Wrap bacon pieces around lamb and secore with toothpicks. Freeze until ready to serve.

For onion soup, heat olive oil in medium sauce pan and over slow heat, saute onions until translucent. Do not brown. Add chicken broth and bring to a boil, add potato. Reduce heat and cover until potato is tender. Place ingredients in bowl of blender. Puree until blended. Strain and add to a clean pan. Add cream and sea salt. Bring to simmer and reduce until slightly thick. Swirl in butter a little at a time.

For garlic glaze, place beef stock and garlic in a saute pan and reduce by half. Add either wine and reduce until slightly thick. Strain Garlic and return to small pan. Heat and swirl in garlic. Reserve and pour over cooked lamb lollipops.

When ready to serve, heat a large saute pan over high heat, add frozen wrapped lamb bacon and cook until bacon is crisp. Remove toothpicks and replace with a lollipop stick. Heat onion soup and pour in a small tall glass container and place cooked lamb lollipop in the soup. Divide lamb glaze over lamb. Season with pepper and enjoy!

Corn Truffle Soup with Corn Fritters

Serves 6-8 | Prep Time 60 | Cook Time 60

WHY I LOVE THIS RECIPE: There is literally nothing that you can't put the taste of truffle on these days. Truffle gives everything an extra sharpness that you never knew you needed. Corn is so sweet and flavorful that when paired with the saltiness of the truffle, it's heaven. I enjoy dipping the corn fritter into the soup as just a small preview of what's to come for the rest of the meal.

INGREDIENTS YOU'LL NEED

Corn Truffle Soup:
3 tablespoons olive oil
4 shallots, minced or 1 large sweet white onion, diced
4 ears of corn, corn removed
2½ cups Chicken Stock or water (see Sauces, Stocks, and Vinaigrettes)
1 teaspoon truffle sea salt
* * *
Corn Fritters:
½ cup flour
1/8 teaspoon baking soda
1/8 teaspoon baking powder
1/4 cup milk or more to make a smooth thick paste
Sea salt to taste
1/3 of remaining corn
2 cups canola oil
Powdered sugar
* * *
3 tablespoons sweet butter
* * *
1 teaspoon truffle oil
1 tablespoon powdered sugar

DIRECTIONS

For Corn Truffle Soup, heat olive oil in a large saucepan over low heat; add shallots and cook for 5 minutes. Add 2/3 of corn and cook over low heat for 10 minutes more. Add Chicken Stock or water. Bring to a boil. Reduce heat and cook for 20 minutes. Cool slightly. Place in blender. Season with salt and blend until very smooth.

For Corn Fritters, mix flour, soda, and baking powder. Whisk in milk and remaining corn. Heat oil to 375 degrees. Drop 1 large tablespoon of batter into oil. Cook until golden on both sides. Drain on towels. Dust with powdered sugar.

When ready to serve, place in clean pot. Heat to boil; reduce heat and stir in butter. Place in cappuccino cup and drizzle truffle oil and powdered sugar on top of Corn Fritters. Serve and enjoy!

Sweet Carrot Cappuccino Soup

Serves 8 | Prep Time 30 | Cook Time 30

WHY I LOVE THIS RECIPE: This soup is DELICIOUS!! Who does not like the sweetness of a fresh organic carrot. They are not only filled with vitamins and carotene , but they are available everywhere. Pair these lovely gems with sauteed onions and some liquid. Puree ingredients and strain and voila you have a fabulous soup. Heat your soup and place in small coffee cups.Next froth some non-fat milk and dollop over hot soup. Top with a little sprinkle of cinnamon and you just might make someone's day that much sweeter.

INGREDIENTS YOU'LL NEED

3½ cups water
or Chicken Stock (see Sauces, Stocks, and Vinaigrettes)
* * *
3 tablespoons olive oil
1 sweet onion, chopped
5 organic carrots, assorted colors if possible, peeled and chopped
1½ teaspoons salt
1 tablespoon sugar
* * *
3 tablespoons sweet butter
½ cup very cold non-fat milk
Dash sugar
Dash salt
2 tablespoons of blanched and minced carrots

DIRECTIONS

Heat olive oil in large saucepan. Add onions and sauté until golden brown. Add carrots and sauté a few minutes. Add reserved Chicken Stock or water, salt, and sugar; bring to boil. Cook for 30 minutes on medium heat. Puree soup a small amount at a time. Strain.

Bring to boil and slowly stir in butter. Whip nonfat milk with dash sugar and dash salt. Set aside. Divide soup among glasses or cappuccino cups. Top with reserved whipped milk and 2 tablespoons assorted minced carrots. Serve and enjoy!

Sweet Pea Soup

Serves 6 | Prep Time 30 minutes | Cook Time 15 minutes

WHY I LOVE THIS RECIPE: Soup is always just a special treat whether it is a first course or a light meal. By adding the garnish of egg, you are giving more protein to this meal. Sugar snap peas focus on color, crunch and added flavors. English peas are becoming more available fresh at all times of the year. Take advantage of their delicious taste and try this recipe. This is one of my dog Desi's favorite treats!

INGREDIENTS YOU'LL NEED

½ cup water

or Vegetable Stock (see Sauces, Stocks, and Vinaigrettes)

* * *

2 cups English peas out of the pod – can be purchased at any market when in season, usually in the winter

6 fresh asparagus cooked, tips reserved for garnish

Sea salt to taste

Freshly ground pepper to taste

* * *

Garnish

1 tables non-fat greek yogurt at room temperature

6 blanched and cut into three pieces, sugar snap peas

Sunny Side-up Quail egg or regular egg.

Pea tendrils and white baby edible flowers optional

6 fresh asparagus tips

DIRECTIONS

Bring 3 cups of water to a strong boil in a large pot. Season with salt and pepper. Add peas and cook about 5 minutes. Drain and place in ice to stop cooking. Puree peas and asparagus in blender and add water or Vegetable Stock to make a smooth and creamy consistency.

Strain. Season with salt and pepper. Heat over low heat and garnish with sugar snap peas and asparagus . Dot with non-fat greek yogurt and optional sunnyside up quail egg. Serve and enjoy!

Lobster Salad with White Beans, Tomatoes, Arugula and Onion Rings

Serves 6 | Prep Time 30 | Cook Time 30

WHY I LOVE THIS RECIPE: What a combination of flavors and textures go into this award-winning salad. Who would not be grateful for having this wonderful meal! Because you are adding beans, you just insured a great natural way to remove plaque in arteries! The more homemade meals you prepare and consume the better you will begin to feel! Enjoy!

INGREDIENTS YOU'LL NEED

Lobster Salad:
3 cups Arugula, torn into small pieces
3 cups Radicchio, torn into small pieces
3 Roma tomatoes, peeled, seeded and diced
1 cup Yellow tomatoes, peeled, seeded and diced
1 cup small white beans, cooked
2 cooked Lobsters, the leg and claws shelled and cut into ½" pieces
Reserve the tail, but slice the tail nearly 1/8" thick
* * *
Seasoned Onion Rings:
1 cup canola oil
½ cup flour
1 teaspoon paprika
1 teaspoon dry mustard
Pinch cayenne pepper
½ teaspoon cumin
2 onions, thinly sliced
Sea salt to taste
* * *
Remoulade Dressing:
1 egg yolk
2 tablespoons agave nectar
1 teaspoon sea salt
¼ cup red wine vinegar
2 tablespoons tomato paste or catsup
1 tablespoon Dijon mustard
1 teaspoon dry mustard
¼ cup water
1 teaspoon Worcester sauce
1 tablespoon sweet relish
2/3 cup canola oil
2 tablespoons Whipped cream, whipped

DIRECTIONS

For Remoulade Dressing, place all ingredients in work bowl of food processor, except oil. Slowly add oil through feed tube. Place in jar and refrigerate until needed. If desired, for every ½ cup dressing, stir in 2 tablespoons whipped cream. For Lobster Salad, combine all ingredients, except the tail of the lobster. Combine with ¾ of the remoulade Dressing. Set aside. For Seasoned Onion Rings, heat oil at 375 degrees. Combine flour, paprika, dry mustard, cayenne pepper, and cumin. Dip sliced onions a few at a time. Shake off excess and cook onions until brown. Place on plate lined with paper towels. Season with sea salt. Set aside. Toss Lobster Salad with some remoulade dressing and place it in individual molds. Spread with a little dressing on top. Arrange reserved lobster tail on top of Lobster Salad and slightly overlap. Garnish with Onion rings. Salad may be dotted with Remoulade Dressing for garnish. Serve and enjoy!

Blackened Tuna Salad with Spicy Soy and Garlic Beurre Blanc

Serves 6 | Prep Time | Cook Time

WHY I LOVE THIS RECIPE: This recipe will instantly take you to the gentle breeze that is Hawaii. When you take the first taste, this tuna will put the biggest smile on your face. Setting the tuna on top of squares of the Japanese sweet potato garnished with the salad is a sure winner! The salad is so great You could have it by itself.

INGREDIENTS YOU'LL NEED

1 large Japanese sweet potato cooked in parchment paper and tin foil. 1 hour 450, reduce heat to 225 and cook one hour more. Turn oven off and let rest in cooled oven for 2 hours.

Salad:
6 Fresh Artichoke hearts, cooked and sliced in half
6 Roma tomatoes, peeled, seeded and diced
36 fresh green beans, blanched
1 cup baby spinach
1 onion, sliced and sautéed in 1 tablespoon olive oil
½ teaspoon sugar
Sea salt
* * *
Spices to blacken tuna:
2 tablespoons paprika
1 tablespoon Dry English mustard
1 teaspoon Chili powder
Ground white pepper
½ teaspoon cumin
* * *
3, four ounce Tuna fillets (cut 1 1/4 thick)
Sea salt
Freshly ground pepper
* * *
Mustard Soy:
1/4 cup English dry mustard
1/3 cup water
½ cup Japanese Rice Vinegar
3 tablespoons Mushroom Soy sauce
1 tablespoon sugar
* * *
White Garlic Beurre Blanc (see recipe in Sauces, Stocks, and Vinaigrettes)
Red Wine Vinaigrette (see recipe in Sauces, Stocks, and Vinaigrettes)

DIRECTIONS

For Salad, combine all ingredients and toss with Red Wine Vinaigrette. Store in bowl in refrigerator until ready to serve. For Spices for tuna, in a bowl, mix all ingredients together. Season Tuna fillets with Spices. Season with sea salt and freshly ground pepper. Refrigerate. For Mustard Soy, in a bowl, combine all ingredients and store in squeeze bottle in refrigerator until ready to use. Heat pan over very high heat. Sear Tuna 2 minutes on each side, thereby blackening the tuna. Slice tuna. Pour White Garlic Beurre Blanc on plate.Place sweet potato on plate and top with tuna, salad, and mustard soy.. Serve and enjoy!

What you are looking for is not out there.....it's in you.

Breads

Banana Flax Pancakes

Serves 2 servings | Prep Time 10 minutes | Cook Time 10 minutes

INGREDIENTS YOU'LL NEED

1/2 cup flax seed meal
1/2 cup hemp seeds
1/4 cup chia seeds
1/4 cup gluten free rolled oats
1/4 cup tapioca flour
1 tsp baking soda
1 tsp. baking powder
1 tsp. Maple syrup
2 dates
2/3 cups coconut milk

DIRECTIONS

In a blender, blend up the dates and coconut milk until the dates are all blended up as much as possible(the milk will be chunky, that's o.k.). Set aside.
In a food processor, pulse the flax, hemp , chia, oats, flour, baking soda and powder until the oats are roughy chopped Pour in a bowl. Add the date milk and maple syrup and stir to combine.
Melt coconut oil (or butter , if you're not vegan) in a non-stick pan. Cook your pancakes in any desired size over medium heat. Flip and cook on the other side. See ve with bananas, cinnamon, and enjoy!

PAIRS WELL WITH: Hot Carob Coconut Milk or Sencha Tea

Brioche

Serves 2 large or 8 sm loaves | Prep Time 20 minutes | Cook Time overnight to rise and 2 hour rise once shaped. 10 to 15 minutes in the oven to bake!

WHY I LOVE THIS RECIPE: "This bread is so wonderful! I use it for hamburger buns sometimes. It is the best for French toast. Just slice when it comes out of the oven with a little jam and it is like going to Paris." When you make your own brioche bread , you are really in for a treat. It is so light and delicious and really so easy to make. Having a Kitchen-Aide Mixer is truly the best way to go. Using the dough hook attachment makes this bread perfect. Give it a try. if freezes so perfectly . You can make it when you have some extra time. Enjoy when you want. have fun!

INGREDIENTS YOU'LL NEED

Please note that part of this recipe needs a lot of time to prepare, so you won't be able to eat this right away.

1 package yeast
4 tablespoons warm water
* * *
2 teaspoons salt
2 tablespoons sugar
1½ tablespoons milk
3¾ cups flour
6 eggs
1 pound butter, take out of refrigerator 15 minutes before you plan to make recipe

DIRECTIONS

Dissolve the yeast in warm water in a bowl. In another bowl, dissolve the salt and sugar into the milk. Place the salt-milk mixture into the bowl of an electric mixer, using the dough hook attachment. Add the flour and the yeast solution and beat for 2 minutes on the low speed. Add 4 eggs all at once and continue to beat until dough is firm and smooth. Add the remaining 2 eggs one at a time. Add the butter a piece at a time. Beat at medium speed until butter is incorporated. Be aware that the dough is very stiff and can cause the machine to move around on the counter. You can purchase rubber grips at specialty stores to help prevent the machine from sliding on the counter.

Place dough in a large bowl and cover with plastic wrap. Let stand at room temperature for 1½ to 2½ hours. When the dough has risen to twice its original size, punch it down and stretch it twice. Let dough rise in the refrigerator for 2 to 3 hours. Punch down and cover tightly with plastic wrap and keep refrigerated overnight. The next day, shape on a cold, floured board. Place in 2 buttered 9 inch loaf pans and let rise 2 to 3 hours at room temperature. Bake at 400 degrees for 25 to 30 minutes. Invert in a cookie sheet. Cool. Serve and enjoy! for smaller loaves, bake 15 to 20 minutes. Dough may also be shaped into balls and placed in a small loaf pan or muffin pan to rise. Bake 450 degree preheated oven for 10 minute

PAIRS WELL WITH: Hot Tea or Cafe Lotte

Challah with Raisins

Serves Makes 2 braided Challahs | Prep Time | Cook Time

WHY I LOVE THIS RECIPE: Challah can easily be substituted for brioche. It does not have as much butter in it and tastes more cake in flavor. My husband loves when I put chocolate chips instead of raisins in the dough before I bake it. The most important thing you need to check for when you make bread, is the expiration date on your yeast. If the yeast is not fresh , your bread will not rise and all your beautiful labors and efforts will go to waste. My friend Ellen, who is a wonderful cook, gave me this recipe and it is the best and very easy to make

INGREDIENTS YOU'LL NEED

1¼ cups very warm water
1 package dry yeast
½ cup sugar plus 1 tablespoon sugar for mixing with the egg and brushing over the challah before it is baked
8½ to 9 cups better for bread flour
4 eggs, room temperature
2 teaspoons salt
1 stick sweet unsalted butter, room temperature
1 cup black or yellow raisins OR 1 ½ cup chocolate chips
1 tablespoon olive oil for bowl

1 egg, room temperature, mixed with 1 tablespoon sugar

DIRECTIONS

Combine water, yeast, and sugar in a large bowl. Let sit for 2 to 5 minutes. Stir in 2 cups flour and let sit covered for 30 minutes. Stir in eggs, salt, butter, 2 more cups flour, and raisins. Mix with a wooden spoon until smooth. Add enough remaining flour to make a soft dough. Turn out the dough on well-floured surface and knead about 10 minutes. Add more flour until dough is no longer sticky. Place dough in a well-oiled bowl. Turn dough once and cover. Let rise 2 hours. Divide dough in half. Cut each half in three pieces and roll each 1/3 into a sausage shape. Attach the three pieces of the dough together at the top. Secure by pressing down on dough with your finger and carefully braid. Do same with other half of dough. To make dough a little higher, you may divide each half into 2/3's, having one piece a little larger for the bottom and top. Each half is then divided into to thirds and braided. The smaller piece goes on top of the larger braided pieces. The dough then rises for two hours before baking.

Turn oven to 350 degrees for a few minutes and turn if off. Place the braid on a cookie sheet and let rise in the turned-off oven for 2 hours.

Brush risen challah with egg-sugar mixture. Preheat oven to 425 degrees and bake about 20 to 25 minutes. Let cool. Serve and enjoy!

Chocolate Cherry Bread

Serves Makes one loaf | Prep Time | Cook Time

WHY I LOVE THIS RECIPE: Chocolate Cherry bread is light and delicious. Eaten right out of the oven, there is absolutely nothing like it. The greatest thing about this bread is that it truly freezes so well. I use it a lot in different recipes and always like to have it on hand. I usually make it on a day when I am not to busy and make about 3 small round loaves from the recipe of 1 large loaf. You will find such satisfaction out of making your own breads. I love the smell of my kitchen when they are baking. Enjoy.

INGREDIENTS YOU'LL NEED

½ package dry yeast
⅔ cups warm water
3 tablespoon honey
3 tablespoons softened sweet unsalted butter
1½ cup good quality cocoa
½ cup chocolate chips
1 cup cherries cooked, recipe in cherry truffles

3 to 4 cups all purpose organic flour
2 teaspoons Himalayan sea salt

1 egg beaten with 1 tablespoon honey

Garnish
cocoa

DIRECTIONS

Pour yeast over ⅔ cups warm water. Let sit for 10 minutes on until bubbles appear. Add ¼ cup of cocoa, ½ cup flour and sugar . Mix thoroughly. Cover bowl with saran wrap and let sit for 1 hour. Stir in remaining ingredients. Knead dough until soft and pliable. Add more flour if to sticky.

Place in a clean lightly oiled bowl. Cover with saran wrap and let rise for 2 hours in a warm turned off oven. If you are making 1 large loaf, wrap into a large 8 inch ball and place on a silpat on a cookie sheet. Flatten a little and place back in a warm turned off oven. Let rise 2 hours more. Dough may also be placed and shaped in small loaf pans or into 3 small rounds.

After rising, bake large loaf in a 400 degree oven for 20 minutes. Let cool and enjoy. Smaller loaves take about 10 minutes. Dust with cocoa and a cherry. Enjoy.

Corn Bread Fingers

Serves Makes about 24 | Prep Time | Cook Time

WHY I LOVE THIS RECIPE: These corn fingers are absolutely addicting. You can find the molds for them in antique shops or go on line. I think the corn fingers bake better when you preheat the mold in the oven for about an hour before baking. I like to fill the batter into a decorating bag and squeeze the batter into the hot buttered molds. They bake quickly and are great to freeze if you do not need right away. I love the addition of fresh corn in the batter. This gives you the added crunch.

INGREDIENTS YOU'LL NEED

½ cup yellow cornmeal or blue cornmeal (for Blue Corn Bread)
½ cup flour
3 tablespoons sugar
1¼ teaspoons baking powder
Dash sea salt
* * *
¼ cup melted butter and extra for mold
1 large egg, separated
3 ears fresh corn, kernels removed and reserved
1/3 cup half and half or heavy cream
1/3 cup milk

DIRECTIONS

Preheat oven to 425 degrees. Put cast iron molds in oven for about 1 hour so that they are very hot.

In a medium bowl, stir together cornmeal, flour, sugar, baking powder, and a dash of sea salt.

In another bowl, combine butter, egg yolk, corn, and half and half or cream and milk.

In yet another bowl, beat egg whites until lightly thick. Combine milk mixture with flour mixture until just combined. Gently fold in beaten egg whites. Place batter in a large pastry bag with ½" tip.

Lightly brush molds with the extra butter. Pipe batter into hot corn molds, ¾ of the way up each mold. Bake 8 to 10 minutes. Cool slightly. Remove corn fingers from oven and place on rack. Place on plates. Serve and enjoy!

PAIRS WELL WITH: Freshly squeezed juices

Homemade Matzos

Serves Makes about 20 Matzohs | Prep Time | Cook Time

WHY I LOVE THIS RECIPE: Matzos are my favorite to make during passover. You can also make the dough gluten free my using a gluten free flour mixture. It is best to put a pizza stone in the lowest part of your oven. preheat it for about 2 hours in a 500 degree oven. Roll the dough out in a pasta machine. Cut with a pizza knife. When you have your matzo shapes ready, just use a fork to make them really look professional. Enjoy!

INGREDIENTS YOU'LL NEED

Egg-Onion:
1 onion, sliced and sautéed in ¼ cup olive oil until golden
1¼ cups Better for Bread flour and extra if needed
1 teaspoon sea salt
* * *
Beet:
1 small fresh beet, cooked
1¼ cups Better for Bread flour and extra if needed
1 teaspoon salt
1 tablespoon olive oil
* * *
Cinnamon Raisin:
¼ cup raisins
1½ teaspoons cinnamon
1¼ cups flour
1 egg white
* * *
Kosher salt

DIRECTIONS

For all the different types of matzohs, place all ingredients in work bowl of food processor. Mix or process until dough forms a ball. Let rest 30 minutes. At this point, the dough may be refrigerated for a few days or frozen for 6 months. Preheat pizza stone in the oven for 2 hours or until very hot. Using a pasta machine, roll out dough until it is very thin. Cut out rectangles and make holes in the rectangles with a fork. If desired, season with a little Kosher salt. Place matzos on stone and bake 60 seconds. Turn and bake 60 seconds more. Serve and enjoy!

PAIRS WELL WITH: Zinfandel or Manischewitz Concord grape Wine

BETTY

Lemon Blueberry and Orange Date Scones

Serves Makes 2 dozen scones | Prep Time | Cook Time

WHY I LOVE THIS RECIPE: A perfect treat with green tea. The batter should be made ahead of time and baked right before you need the scones. Lemon blueberry is our families favorite. You can use any fruit however with perfect results. They are delicious and very easy to make. I love that you can freeze for later use as needed. I have also added a recipe for my favorite and very easy jam. You can substitute any fruit you like and have the same great results. You may also change the flavor of the scones by adding dates and orange or any flavor you like. They will be wonderful. Also making the dough in advance and freezing is great. You can cut the scones in any shape you like. Hearts are wonderful for Valentine's day or a bridal shower. Cut what you need and bake fresh every time. Scones are really more like a biscuit. When I roll them out, I do it on a frozen plastic cutting board. By freezing the board, it allows you to use less flour which will make the scones taste more flaky and delicious.

INGREDIENTS YOU'LL NEED

3 cups cake flour
Extra flour for rolling
2 tablespoons baking powder
3 tablespoons sugar
¾ teaspoon salt
1 stick sweet butter, cut into cubes
1¾ cups whipping cream (and extra if needed)
1 cup blueberries, dried
2 tablespoons lemon peel, grated
* * *
Strawberry Jam:
2 cups sugar
2 cups water
6 cups beautifully ripe strawberries
* * *
1 egg yolk, beaten

DIRECTIONS

Sift together flour, baking powder, sugar, and salt. Use paddle on electric mixer to work butter into flour mixture until mealy. Add whipping cream, blueberries, and lemon peel. Mix on low until smooth, about 1 minute.

For Strawberry Jam, bring sugar and water to boil over high heat. Boil until sugar dissolves in water. Let cool. Slice off the tops of the strawberries. Place strawberries into large bowl. Pour sugar/water mixture over top and cover tightly with plastic wrap. Marinate for 3 days at room temperature. This will bring the natural pectin out of the fruit. Pour strawberries and liquid into a large 12-inch non-stick pan. Bring mixture to a boil and reduce heat. Simmer until thick. Pour into jars. Cool and cover. Refrigerate.

Turn dough onto a cold floured board and roll to about ¾" thick. With pastry cutter, cut dough into 1¼" rounds. Place dough on parchment-lined cookie sheet and bake at 375 degrees until golden brown. Brush with egg yolk. Bake 12 to 15 minutes. Serve with fresh strawberry jam. Enjoy!

Orange Brioche French Toast

Serves 6 | Prep Time 20 | Cook Time 5

WHY I LOVE THIS RECIPE: "When we first received the call that we might have to evacuate, it seemed unimaginable until I looked out the window at the smoke whirling across the beautiful morning. We called our friends Carole and Marty, and Harriet and Steven, to see how they were as they were closer to it." This is a very elegant, yet satisfying brunch dish. This recipe can also be served as a great desert. I always make my brioche bread a day when I am in the mood and have time. I always like to have this bread in my freezer as it is so versatile. The first time you make your own brioche and slice it is a spiritual experience. I still remember it to this day. You feel you are in heaven. Have fun!

INGREDIENTS YOU'LL NEED

6 eggs
½ cup half and half
1/8 cup sugar
2 tablespoons Grand Marnier
1 tablespoon orange peel, grated
* * *
6 1 ½ " thick slices of Brioche, cut on the diagonal.
Please note that making the Brioche should be made in advance. You may freeze the loaves and use when needed.

Brioche Recipe
1 package yeast
2 teaspoons warm water

2 teaspoons salt
2 tablespoons sugar
1½ tablespoons milk
3¾ cups flour
6 eggs
1 pound butter, room temperature
* * *
Ganache:
6 ounces white chocolate or dark chocolate
¼ cup heavy cream
* * *
Chocolate Sauce – this makes 1 cup, but only ½ cup is needed here. You can refrigerate remaining sauce and use another time:
3½ ounces semi-sweet chocolate
6 tablespoons milk
1 tablespoon heavy cream

5 tablespoons granulated sugar
1 tablespoon butter
* * *
3 tablespoons sweet butter
* * *
Powdered sugar, sifted
Whipped cream and
½ cup pure maple syrup

DIRECTIONS

Mix together eggs, half and half, sugar, Grand Marnier and orange peel. Set aside.

Make brioche in advance. You may purchase brioche in a fine bakery but making your own is the best. For the Brioche, dissolve the yeast in warm water in a bowl. In another bowl, dissolve the salt and sugar into the milk. Place the salt-milk mixture into the bowl of an electric mixer, using the dough hook attachment. Add the flour and the yeast solution and beat for 2 minutes on the low speed. Add 4 eggs all at once and continue to beat until dough is firm and smooth. Add the remaining 2 eggs one at a time. Add the butter a piece at a time. Beat at medium speed until butter is incorporated. Be aware that the dough is very stiff and can cause the machine to move around on the counter. You can purchase rubber grips at specialty stores to help prevent the machine from sliding on the counter. You can also roll a large dishtowel into a circle with space in the middle to keep machine from sliding.

Place dough in a large bowl and cover with plastic wrap. Let stand at room temperature for 1½ to 2½ hours. When the dough has risen to twice its original size, punch it down and stretch it twice. Let dough rise in the refrigerator for 2 to 3 hours. Punch down and cover tightly with plastic wrap and keep refrigerated overnight.

The next day, shape on a cold, floured board. Place in 2 buttered 9 inch loaf pans and let rise 2 to 3 hours at room temperature. Brush with remaining 1 egg.Bake at 400 degrees for 25 to 30 minutes. Invert onto a cake rack. You can also make muffins with this recipe. Butter miniature or regular muffin tins. Shape dough into either a large or small ball.With your fingers delicately making a small ball shape on top of a larger one.Place in muffin tins and let them rise1 ½ to 2 ½ hours. Small muffins take 8 to 10 minutes. Larger muffins about 15 minutes

Slice 6, 1 inch slices out of brioche bread. Cut each piece in half. Pour prepared egg mixture over sliced bread in pan. Marinate for 1 hour or overnight if desired.

For Ganache, place white chocolate or dark chocolate in food processor. Heat cream to boil. Slowly pour hot cream over chocolate while machine is running, place in a bowl and set aside.

For Chocolate Sauce, melt chocolate in double boiler or in microwave oven. In saucepan, bring milk to boil. Add the heavy cream and bring back to a boil. Remove pan from heat and stir in sugar, melted chocolate, and butter. Replace pot on heat and boil the sauce for a few seconds. Strain into a container and cool. Refrigerate until ready to use. Warm slightly before serving.

Spread one slice brioche with ganache and place the other half on top. Place sandwiched brioches into egg mixture.

When ready to serve, heat butter in large non-stick pan. When butter is very brown, add Brioche and cook until golden brown on each side. Spread one slice brioche with ganache and top with another cooked brioche. Continue with other brioche spreading and layering. Remove to plate. Garnish with powdered sugar, whipped cream, maple syrup, and chocolate sauce. Serve and enjoy!

Truffle Pizza with Mascarpone and White Truffle

Serves 1 Pizza | Prep Time 10 minutes | Cook Time 12 minutes

WHY I LOVE THIS RECIPE: This gives pizza a brand new meaning. The mascarpone truffle filling is the absolute best. The topping of 5 different cheeses melting into the wonderful truffle sauce and then to top it off, a drizzle of truffle honey. You will never see pizza in the same way! If summer black truffles or white truffles are available , by all means shave them over the top. You can purchase these at farmers market or a gourmet cheese store. Always make the dough for the pizza when you have time. It can be divided into portions and placed in freezer bags and frozen for months.

INGREDIENTS YOU'LL NEED

Dough – makes 6-8 pizzas, freeze remaining dough:
1 package dry yeast
1¼ cups warm water
1 tablespoon agave nectar, sugar, or honey
1 tablespoon olive oil
1 teaspoon salt
4 cups organic bread flour
* * *
Filling:
½ cup Mascarpone cheese
1½ cups Parmesan cheese
2 tablespoons truffle oil
½ teaspoon truffle salt
* * *
Topping:
¼ pound Jack cheese, thinly sliced
¼ pound Muenster cheese, thinly sliced
¼ pound Mozzarella cheese, thinly sliced
¼ pound brie cheese or truffle cheese, hard crust removed, sliced as thinly as you can
¼ ounce Alba white truffle, thinly sliced, optional
2 tablespoons truffle honey

DIRECTIONS

For Dough, sprinkle yeast over warm water, agave nectar, olive oil, salt and dissolved yeast. Place flour in bowl and mix in yeast mixture. Knead and cover in clear bowl. Let rise 1 hour.

For Filling, combine all ingredients. Set aside and let rest 5 minutes.

Preheat pizza stone to 500 degrees. Roll Pizza Dough very thin. Sprinkle with some corn meal. Using 1/6 of the pizza dough, roll out very thin. Place rolled out dough on the corn meal paddle. Place mascarpone mixture on dough and top with the cheese. You may roll the edges around the pizza up to 1 inch. Slide the pizza onto the hot pizza sone in oven. Close door and bake 500 degrees for about 8 to 19 minutes. Check to see that the cheese is melting and the crust is golden brown. Remove with metal paddle. Enjoy!

Poached Baby Quail Eggs on Miniature Brioche with Truffle Sauce

Serves 8 | Prep Time 30 minutes | Cook Time 30 minutes

WHY I LOVE THIS RECIPE: This was really my son Ryan's favorite breakfast growing up. I would substitute the truffles for caviar. My older son Ryan had his first taste of caviar at age 3 when my wonderful mother-in-law decided she would share her gift of caviar from a friend with us. He was hooked on it from the beginning. Like older brother ,Chad, my second son loved it too! When truffles are not in season, caviar is.

INGREDIENTS YOU'LL NEED

1 tablespoon vinegar
8 quail eggs
* * *
Truffle Sauce:
½ cups Chicken Stock (see Sauces, Stocks, and Vinaigrettes)
½ Pinot Grigio white wine
1 shallot diced
¼ cup heavy organic cream
1 sprig thyme
2 tablespoons sweet organic butter
1/4 teaspoon truffle salt
* * *
8 miniature Brioche, may be made in advance. See recipe for broiche bread in recipe for brioche bread

Garnish
1 tablespoon Chives, sprinkled on top of each serving
1 summer black truffle sliced thin

DIRECTIONS

Bring a large saucepan of water, almost to the top, to a boil. Add vinegar. Carefully break 1 quail egg into a small cup. Do same with the other eggs, each placed in their own cup. Reduce heat. Slide each quail egg into the hot vinegar water from its own small dish, cooking one at a time. Cook for one minute, placing hot water from the poaching water over top to cook. Remove to bowl of water and continue with remaining eggs. Eggs can now stay until ready to serve.

For truffle sauce, place chicken broth, white wine and shallot in a small saucepan. Bring to a boil and reduce mixture to 1 tablespoon. Place that 1 tablespoon in a small saucepan and add cream. Bring to a simmer and simmer to blend flavors. When ready to serve. Bring that mixture to a simmer again and stir in butter a little at a time. Season with 1/4 teaspoon of truffle salt.

Heat quail eggs , if made ahead, pour warm water over and let stay for 2 minutes. Remove from water and place egg on toasted 1//2 on brioche muffin and divide sauce over each egg. Place some optional chives over place top over egg and enjoy.

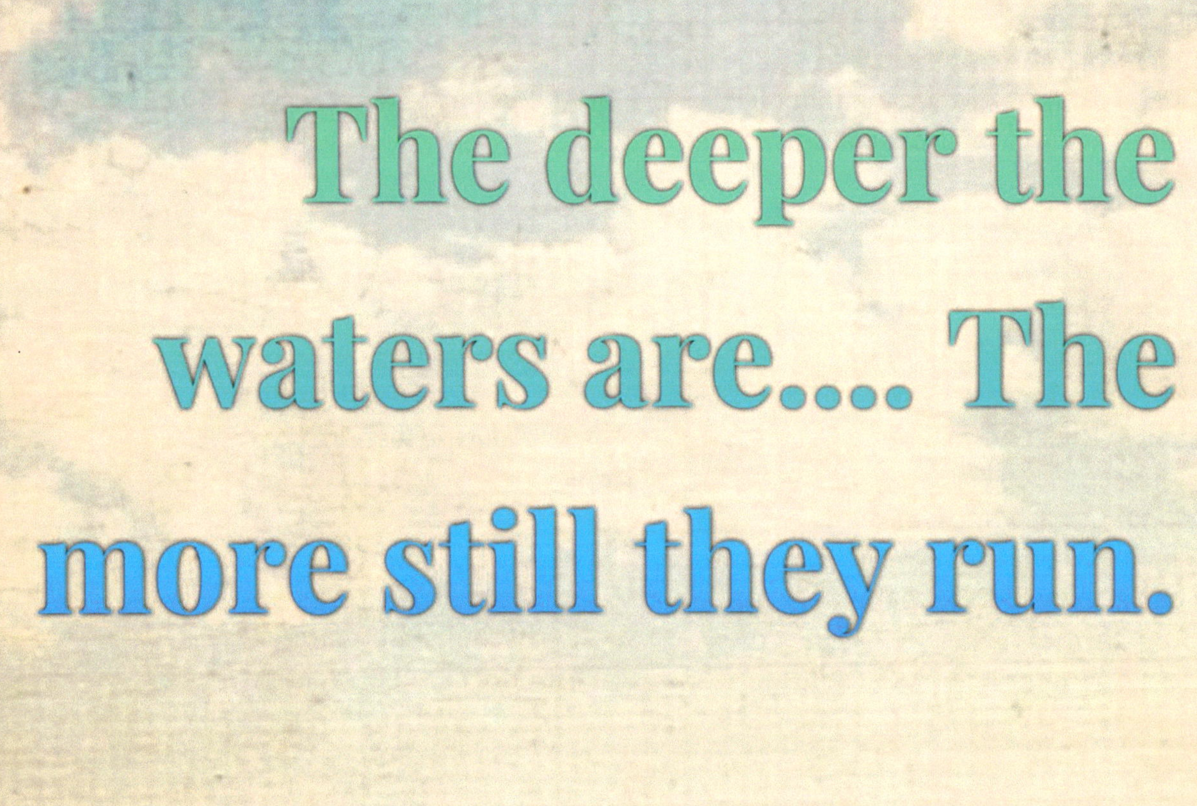
The deeper the
waters are.... The
more still they run.

Pasta and Hispanic Fusion

Sweet Corn Tamales by Gina Burrell

Serves 8 | Prep Time 3 hours | Cook Time Tamales, from start to finish about 1 hour. Salsa will take 15 minutes

WHY I LOVE THIS RECIPE: "Having grown up in México City, these were a staple in our house. They are especially eaten at Christmas, but are great any time of the year." Great tamales. Delicious, and will be enjoyed by all. These were a staple in my family. We ate them all year long, though traditionally they are made for Christmas.

INGREDIENTS YOU'LL NEED

TAMALES

38. Ears fresh corn
2lbs. Monterrey Jack Cheese - grated
1 cup. Yellow Corn Meal
1 Jalapeño chile - finely chopped
1 Tbl. Kosher salt
Sour cream for garnish
1 Pkg. Dried corn husks (can purchase in a Mexican Market)

GREEN TOMATILLO SALSA

Makes 2 1/2 cups
3/4 cup Chicken stock - preferably homemade
1 sml. onion - coarsely chopped
1 lb. Fresh green tomatillos - husked and quartered
(when buying, open skins and make sure there are no blemishes)
2 Jalapeño chiles - finely chopped (or to taste)
2 Medium garlic cloves minced
1 Bunch cilantro, coarse stems removed - chopped
1/4 tsp. Cumin seed. (roast in a dry pan until fragrant)
1/2 tsp. Kosher salt (or to taste)
1 Tbl. Fresh lemon juice
2 cups. Sour cream

DIRECTIONS

TAMALES

Clean dried husks (remove silks), and soak in hot water for about 1 hour.

Clean corn - cut kernels off of cobs and discard cobs. In a food processor, fitted with the steel blade, process 4 cups of kernels with a handful cheese and some cornmeal, until completely pureed. Pour into a large mixing bowl, and continue processing corn and cheese and cornmeal, until all has. been pureed. Add the chile and salt to taste, and mix well.

Take husks and pat dry. From the small husks, shred off. long pieces for tying of the tamales. Lay 2 husks on a work surface with the 2 wide ends overlapping. Spoon about 1/4 cup mixture in center of husks. DO NOT OVERFILL, as filling will expand during the cooking process. Also remember, that the amount of the filling depends on the size of the husks.

Take the side of the husk nearest to you, and roll it into the opposite direction, doing the same with the other side, encasing the filling. Tuck tail ends over and form a nice little package. Take one of the pieces of shredded husk to tie the package together. Place seam side down on a steamer lined with tamale husks. (You can get inexpensive large steamers at Mexican markets, or in a Chinese market). These freeze beautifully once cooked, then to re-heat, simply remove from the freezer - do not defrost, and steam until hot.

SALSA
In a large skillet heat the chicken stock over medium heat. Simmer covered the onion in the chicken stock for about 5 minutes. Add the tomatillos, and cook covered for another 5 minutes.

Pour the contents of the skillet into a blender and process until coarsely chopped. Be careful processing a hot liquid, as the top can explode. Hold top down firmly with a towel covering it. Add the chiles, garlic, cilantro, cumin, salt and lemon juice. Taste and adjust the seasonings.

You can refrigerate the sauce at this point for up to 3-5 days. When. ready to serve with the tamales, take 3/4 cup tomatillo sauce and blend with 2 cups of sour cream.

*Note - once you add the sour cream, the sauce will be less spicy.

Enjoy!

Mich's Spinach Gnocchi

Serves 6 to 8 as a first course | Prep Time 25 minutes | Cook Time 10 minutes

WHY I LOVE THIS RECIPE: This recipe is from Chris Reed. Chris says, "On November 8th 2018 we were home and then we evacuated to Palm Springs on 9/11. The spinach gnocchi is a Roman recipe that my ex-wife Mich, used to make to perfection. She would drop the gnocchi's into the boiling water. They were ready when they rose to the surface. The joke here is that, at this stage of the recipe , she would call that the Ascension of Testi". Enjoy

INGREDIENTS YOU'LL NEED

1/2 cup chopped cooked spinach, squeezed dry
3/4 cups sheep milks ricotta
5 tablespoons all purpose organic flour, plus 1/2 cup or more for rolling out gnocchi.
1 eggs
3/4 cup reggiano parmesan cheese
1 teaspoon sea salt
grating of nutmeg
1 teaspoon grated onion optional

Sauce
6 tablespoons sweet butter
5 to 6 fresh sage leaves, torn in half
sea salt
1 tablespoon honey

DIRECTIONS

Combine all ingredients and roll into a 1 inch oval. Drop into boiling and salted water. When they rise place on warm plates and pour browned sage butter over and enjoy!

For browned sage butter , heat butter in a small sauce pan and heat until lightly brown Add sage leaves and honey. Season with sea salt.

PAIRS WELL WITH: Burgundy

Pastel de Tortilla by Gina Burrell

Serves 4 to 6 servings | Prep Time 30 minutes | Cook Time 30 minutes

WHY I LOVE THIS RECIPE: "I was born and raised in Mexico City and this was one of my most favorite dishes we made." Gina Burrell is an incredible cook and person , She worked on the first cookbook for Malibu, "Malibu's Cooking Again". She was very instrumental in getting so many wonderful recipes and stories added to this book. The world is better for her being in it.

INGREDIENTS YOU'LL NEED

SAUCE

2 cups chicken broth (homemade is best) use a fresh made chicken broth you make or purchase fresh at market (Erewhon is a good source)

1 ` 1/2 pounds green tomatillos- check under the papery skin to make sure there are no blemishes- husked and rinsed

1-2 Serrano peppers(or to taste)

1/2 sliced sweet white onion

2 garlic cloves peeled

1/2 bunch fresh cilantro - cut off the tough stems

3/4 cup sour cream

2 tablespoons canola oil

* * *

PASTEL

12 day old tortillas

3/4 cups canola oil

1 whole skinless chicken breast cut in. half, poached in chicken broth, cooled and shredded

2 cups shredded Mexican Oaxaca cheese or Monterrey Jack cheese

* * *

SALAD

1 cup baby spinach

1 cup baby shredded cilantro

1/2 baby edible flowers

2 tablespoons mustard vinaigrette

DIRECTIONS

For the tomatillo sauce, in a heavy non-reactive 6 quart sauce pan over medium heat, add 4 cups of water and add the cleaned tomatillos, the chilies, the garlic and the onion. Bring to a boil. Reduce heat to a simmer, until the tomatillos are tender- about 10-12 minutes. Drain. Place tomatillos, onion, garlic and cilantro in a blender with one chile and some salt to taste. If not hot enough add second chile. Blend until thoroughly smooth. If seeming too thick, add some chicken broth. Add sour cream to sauce. Taste and adjust seasoning. Place in a heavy 12-inch skillet with deep sides and heat over medium low heat and cook for about 10 minutes. Stir often. Reserve.

Prepare your baking casserole (a soufflé dish works perfectly) Lightly oil casserole and reserve. In a heavy 10-inch skillet, heat the oil over medium heat until the oil shimmers. Using tongs, submerge the tortillas , one at a time into the hot oil for about 10 seconds. (tortillas must be pliable). Place on paper towels to absorb oil. Add a little sauce to your prepared casserole and add a tortilla to the pan. Top with more sauce ,a little chicken, and cheese. Keep layering ending with a tortilla ,some sauce and top with cheese.. Cover tightly with parchment and then aluminum foil. Refrigerate overnight so flavors can meld. Next day, bring out of refrigerator, bring to room temperature. Bake in a 350 degree oven for 30 minutes or until edges are lightly browned. Let cool and slice. Top with salad of spinach , cilantro and baby flowers tossed in balsamic vinaigrette. Enjoy!

Tomato Pearl Pasta with Fried Spinach

Serves 6 | Prep Time 30 minutes | Cook Time 10 minutes

WHY I LOVE THIS RECIPE: This pesto recipe is a little more traditional. Always make sure your basil is beautiful and green. Never use the stems in making a pesto as this will discolor your pesto and make it brown. Pearl pasta is sometimes called Israeli couscous and can be found in most ethnic markets. Putting the tomato sauce and the fried spinach as a topping is a very delicious combination of flavors. Try for yourself and see.

INGREDIENTS YOU'LL NEED

Pesto:
2 fresh garlic cloves
½ cup pine nuts
2 cups Fresh basil leaves
1 teaspoon sea salt
½ cup olive oil
1½ cups fresh grated Parmesan cheese
* * *
Tomato Sauce (see Sauces, Stocks, and Vinaigrettes)
½ cup Pearl Pasta – this recipe makes 1½ cups pasta. You may freeze unused portion and use another time:
1/4 cup olive oil
2 shallots, diced
1 cup Chicken Stock (see Sauces, Stocks, and Vinaigrettes)
1 cup water
1/4 teaspoon salt
1 recipe tomato sauce
¼ cup Parmesan cheese
2 tablespoons butter
2 Shallots, chopped
2 tablespoons olive oil
2 garlic cloves, minced
1 ripe tomato, chopped
½ cup Tomato Sauce (see Sauces, Stocks, and Vinaigrettes)
1¼ cups Chicken Stock (see Sauces, Stocks, and Vinaigrettes)
Sea salt to taste
Dash crushed red pepper
* * *
Fried Spinach Chips
36 baby spinach leaves washed and thoroughly dried
1 cup non-gmo canola oil
Sea salt to taste

DIRECTIONS

For Pesto, in work bowl of food processor, finely chop garlic and pine nuts. Add basil leaves and process until all ingredients are pureed. Add salt and olive oil until very finely pureed. Store in container in refrigerator until ready to use. Serve at room temperature. For Pearl Pasta, heat olive oil in a small saucepan. Sauté shallots until translucent. Add pearl pasta and sauté a few minutes more. Add reserved Chicken Stock, water, and salt; bring to boil and then reduce heat. Cover and simmer 30 minutes or until tender. Stir in tomato sauce, and lastly the butter. Set aside. For fried spinach, heat canola oil in pan to 325 degrees. Add spinach and fry until translucent and crisp. Drain on paper towel and season with sea salt. Reserve. Divide pasta among plates. Brush plate with tomato sauce. Dot with some pesto sauce. Grate some parmesan cheese over. Garnish with spinach leaves. Serve and enjoy!

Carla Bowman Smith's Chicken Enchilada Casserole

Serves 4 to 6 servings | Prep Time 25 minutes | Cook Time 30 minutes

WHY I LOVE THIS RECIPE: "A simple recipe. This is one of my families favorite recipes. Easy to make and truly delicious." Carla said this is how the fire impacted their lives. Carla grew up in Malibu and after college, moved back into her families home on Cavalleri. Her grandparents Enrico and Inez Cavalleri moved to Malibu in 1942. Later Portshead Road was named after their son, my uncle, Louis Cavalleri. The day of the fire we evacuated to Zuma Beach with my dog Sizzles and our tortoise. I escaped with my late father-in-laws Leica Camera and our tax papers. Stan was able to take his late father's horn and Stephen took his xbox. We brought a change of clothes but fully expecting to be back the next day at the latest. Growing up in Malibu, I had been through multiple evacuations, always able to come home, and did not expect this time would be any different. But it was. Everything was lost. Our home and 3 rentals, a major part of our income. People who haven't lost everything, say, well it's just stuff, but it really isn't. We lost mementoes that we can never get back. A storybook with my late mother's voice recorded on it reading to my brother, their wedding album, family photos, furniture that my late father built and my son's baby teeth. But we are also blessed with our community and surrounding communities support. Strangers making sure that we had clothes, neighbors welcoming us into their home, letting us know they cared, meant the world to us and helps fill the emptiness we felt.

INGREDIENTS YOU'LL NEED

Cut meat from 1 small chicken
3 cups shredded cheddar
2 small cans sliced olives or 40 fresh kalamata olives sliced thin
1 jar Salsa Verde (Trader Joe's works well , says Carla
15 corn tortillas

Homemade Salsa Verde
1 1/2 pounds tomatillos
1/2 cup chopped white onions
5 cloves garlic
1 cup cilantro leaves
1 tablespoon lime juice
1 or 2 serrano pepper, seeded and chopped
salt to taste

DIRECTIONS

Preheat oven to 400 degrees. I na large casserole dish put some salsa to cover bottom with a this layer.Put a layer of tortillas, tear torillas as necessary to fit the casserole bottom. Pour some of the salsa on tortillas then layer with chicken and cheese. Sprinkle with some olives. Then repeat with tortillas, salsa , chicken, cheese and olives until finished with ingredients. Top with more salsa and remaining cheese and olives. Cook 30 minutes. Serve warm and enjoy!

For salsa, cook tomatillos in water . Bring to a boil and cook with onions for 10 to 15 minutes. Remove and drain liquid. Place in blender with garlic, cilantro, lime and jalapeño. Season with salt to taste. Puree un til well blended. Reserve.

Yellow Corn Polenta with Strawberry Garlic Sauce

Serves 6-8 | Prep Time 30 minutes | Cook Time 30 minutes

WHY I LOVE THIS RECIPE: This recipe is sure to be a crowd pleaser. you can actually use any fruit you like that is in season. Berries work wonderfully too. I love white peaches when they are in season. We have been blessed in Malibu with our own white peach tree. If we can get there before the squirrels , we are grateful!

INGREDIENTS YOU'LL NEED

1 3/4 cups chicken broth or more
1 cup water
1 cup corn polenta
1/4 teaspoon Himalayan Salt

Strawberry garlic sauce

12 strawberries coarsely chopped
1 tablespoon honey
1/4 teaspoon chopped red chili pepper
3 cloves fresh garlic
sea salt to taste
1/2 cup water
1/3 cup olive oil

DIRECTIONS

Bring 1 1/2 cups chicken broth and water to a boil. Reduce heat and gradually add polenta. Stir until liquid is absorbed. Keep adding more liquid every 5 minutes or so until mixture cooks for about 30 minutes. You can continue to cook longer , adding more liquid as need. Season to taste with some Himalayan salt.

Make strawberry garlic sauce. Place all ingredients in a skillet , bring to a boil and reduce heat. Cook until sauce it thickens slightly. Stir in olive oil and cook a few moments more. Place polenta in each plate and grate some parmesan over top. Divide strawberry sauce over. Season with a little freshly ground pepper. Serve and enjoy.

Tortellini with Beets in Pesto Sauce

Serves 10 | Prep Time 30 minutes | Cook Time 10 minutes

WHY I LOVE THIS RECIPE: The beautiful color of the fresh beets coming through the pasta blended with the delicious pesto butter is memorable in your mouth. The dough may be made well in advance. The tortellini's can be made ahead and frozen. Even the pesto butter can stay in the freezer. When you are ready to serve, just make the wine reduction and stir in the pesto butter, strain, and place in a pan. Add the cooked tortellini and you are ready for a treat!

INGREDIENTS YOU'LL NEED

Pasta Dough – use half for this recipe and freeze remaining for another time:
¾ cup flour
¼ cup Semolina flour
1 egg
1 tablespoon Virgin olive oil
½ teaspoon salt
1 tablespoon or more water
Egg white for brushing
* * *
Filling:
1 small red beet cooked and peeled
1/3 cup Mascarpone cheese
1/4 cup grated Parmesan cheese
1/4 teaspoon sea salt
Freshly ground pepper to taste
* * *
½ cup white wine
2 shallots
½ cup Chicken Stock (see Sauces, Stocks, and Vinaigrettes)
* * *
Pesto Butter
1 stick butter softened
1 teaspoon Himalayan salt
7 garlic cloves
2 cups fresh basil

DIRECTIONS

For pesto butter, combine garlic and basil in the work bowl of the food processor. When mixture is finely chopped to a puree, add butter and salt. Shape into a log and freeze until needed.

For Pasta dough, combine all ingredients in food processor, except for the egg white used for brushing, until smooth dough is formed. Add more water or flour, depending on the consistency. Roll pasta dough through pasta machine until long and thin. Use flour as needed to prevent sticking. Cut into 1½ inch squares. Place 1/4 teaspoon beet filling in the center of each rectangle. Brush with egg white around edges. Fold carefully over to secure edges. Press ends together. Place on floured lined tin foil on a cookie sheet or large plate. Repeat with remaining pasta. Let dry on one side and turn over to allow the other side to dry. Tortellini may be frozen for a later use. Place in baggies.

For Filling, place beets in the work bowl of the food processor and process until finely pureed. Add Mascarpone cheese, Parmesan cheese, salt and pepper. Process until mixture is well combined. Set aside.

Place wine, shallots and Chicken Stock in a small saucepan. Bring to a boil and reduce mixture by half. Strain and discard shallots. Place reduced liquid in a clean saucepan. Set aside.

When ready to serve, bring a large skillet to a boil. Season with sea salt and 1 tablespoon of olive oil. Place prepared tortellini into boiling water and cook on a low heat for about 10 minutes or until tender. Place reserved pesto butter in a non-stick skillet. Add tortellini and cook over low heat. I like to serve 3 to 5 tortellinis per person. Grate some parmesan cheese over and enjoy.

Place reduced chicken broth and wine into a small saucepan. Bring to a boil and reduce heat. Slowly mix in basil butter, 1 tablespoon at a time. Strain into a non-stick skillet. Then add tortellini.

HAVE FAITH......
A LOT CAN
HAPPEN IN A YEAR

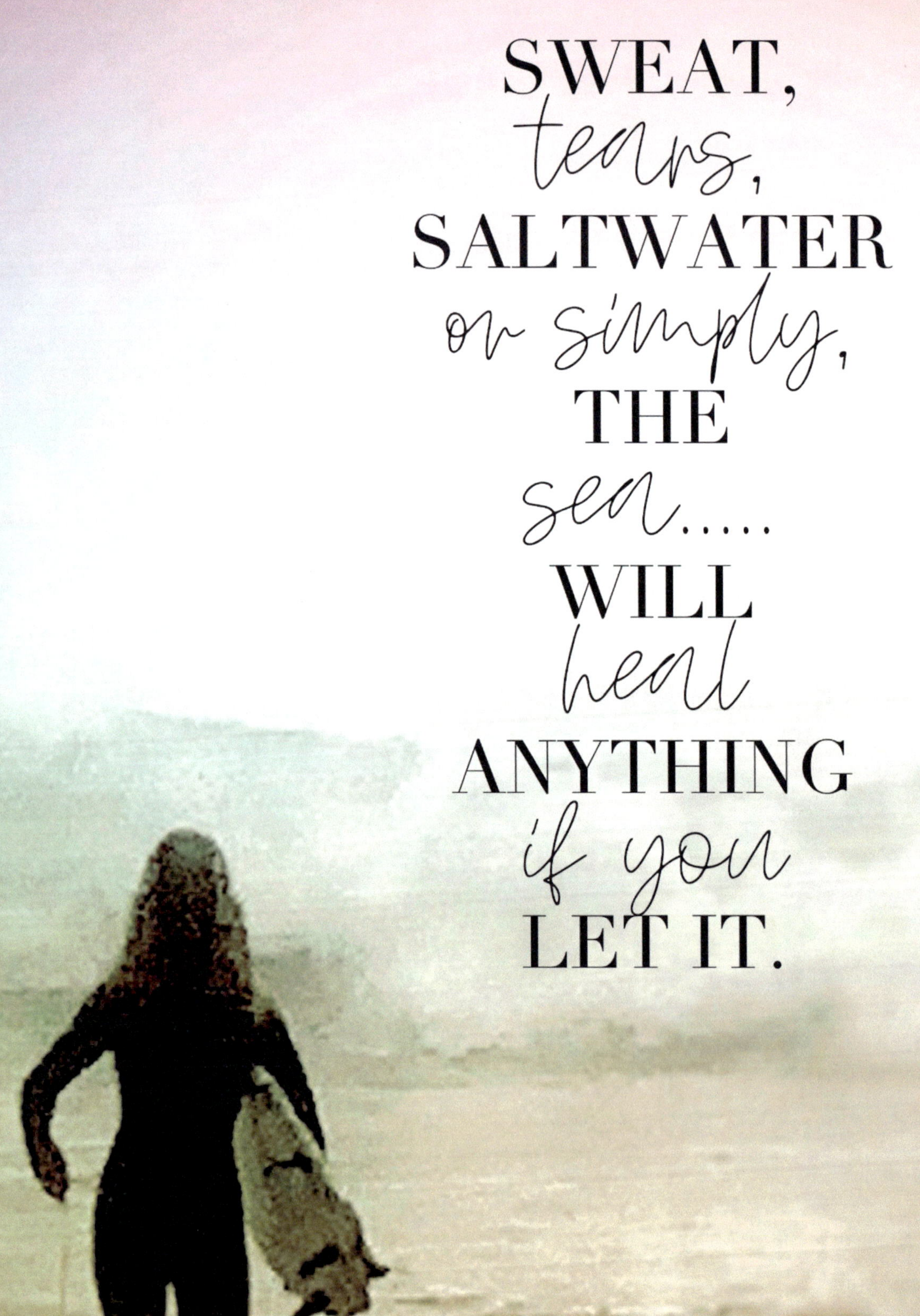
SWEAT,
tears,
SALTWATER
or simply,
THE
sea.....
WILL
heal
ANYTHING
if you
LET IT.

Main Courses

Black Tie Turkey

Serves 10 to 12 | Prep Time | Cook Time

WHY I LOVE THIS RECIPE: This turkey will delight your entire family and friends. When this guy comes to the table dressed in his vest and bow tie, everyone will do a double take. The vest is made out of flaky puff pastry. I love to make my own puff pastry when I have time and just keep it in the freezer when I need it. It can also be purchased at finer bakeries and at some speciality markets in the freezer section. Try to buy puff pastry made with butter. You may design the vest anyway you like. You may even want to dress this turkey as a girl. Just have fun!

INGREDIENTS YOU'LL NEED

For clothes, measure turkey while it is still cold. Place wax paper over top and trace with pencil. Make a few lines. With the edge of your fingers, place pattern over puff pastry.

Puff Pastry, about ½ pound (also called Detrempe, may be purchased at supermarkets)
½ pound bread flour
½ pound all-purpose unbleached flour
3 ounces sweet butter, chilled and cut into 6 pieces
Pinch salt
1 cup ice water

1¼ pounds sweet butter, chilled
¼ cup unbleached flour
* * *
Stuffing
½ stick sweet butter
3 tablespoons olive oil
3 portobello mushrooms, chopped
Sea salt to taste
Freshly ground pepper to taste

3 onions, chopped
1 fennel bunch, chopped
½ head garlic (10 to 15 garlic cloves), mashed
3 cups sourdough bread, diced

3 tablespoons olive oil
1 fresh turkey, 15 to 16 pounds
Sea salt to taste
Pepper to taste
1 stick sweet butter
1 garlic head, peeled and minced
3 carrots , peeled and chopped
3 celery stalks , peeled and chopped
1 red onion peeled and chopped
8 whole garlic cloves unpeeled
Reserved neck of turkey

For Clothes
String to hold legs together
2 egg yolks
Black and Red food coloring
½ stick sweet butter

DIRECTIONS

If making your own puff pastry or Detrempe, place all ingredients, except the iced water, into work bowl of food processor. Remove the Detrempe from refrigerator. Cut a deep cross in the dough. Spread out the sections of the dough so that the center is the thickest part. Roll the dough out from each section to form a four leaf clover. Try to keep the center a little thicker. Place the butter in the center and bring the edges of the Detrempe to the center. It is like enclosing the butter in an envelope. Cover pastry with plastic wrap or tin foil. Chill 1 hour. Roll pastry into a 9" by 12' rectangle on a frozen plastic board, fold in thirds and roll again to 9" by 12 " rectangle. Fold into thirds and refrigerate. Repeat this process two more times. Maybe frozen at this point. Cut into smaller portions and freeze. Place in refrigerator to thaw before using.

Preheat oven to 350 degrees. Roll out ¼" thick Puff Pastry on cold cutting board. Place pattern over make clothes according to pattern, as explained in beginning of recipe. To make Stuffing, heat butter and olive oil and sauté portobello mushrooms until golden. Season with sea salt and freshly ground pepper. Remove from pan. In another pan, add onions and fennel to pan and sauté until golden brown; add garlic. Sauté a few minutes more. Mix in bread cubes and mushrooms. Season with sea salt and pepper. Set aside.

Season turkey with sea salt and pepper. First mix garlic with sweet butter, simmer to blend flavors. Pour over inside and over top of turkey. Stuff turkey. Tie turkey legs together with string. Cook turkey breast side down on rack. Place onion chopped, carrots, celery , turkey neck and garlic under rack of turkey. After the turkey has been baking for 1 hour, pan juices and cook 45 minutes more.Turn over and return to oven, baste it with the garlic and butter mixture from juices from turkey and continue baking for 15 to 20 minutes or until golden brown . Turkey should bake 12 to 15 minutes per pound.

While turkey is baking, prepare the Clothes: tuxedo, bow tie, and shirt. Mix black food colorings with egg yolk. Mix red food coloring with another egg yolk. Paint vest in black and red stripes. Paint bow tie red. Paint black studs on cuff, like cufflinks. Refrigerate clothes.

Gravy for turkey
2 tablespoons organic flour
10 thyme sprigs
1 cup madeira wine
2 cups chicken stock
Water

Thirty minutes before turkey is finished baking, remove from oven. Cool slightly. Increase oven temperature to 425 degrees. Place clothes on turkey. Bake dressed turkey until pastry is golden, about 10 not 15 minutes. Remove and let rest 25 minutes before carving.

For gravy, while turkey is resting, remove all oil except 3 tablespoons. Discard vegetables Mix oil with 2 tablespoon organic flour and mix together for a few minutes. Add 1/2 cup Madeira wine. Bring to a boil and add 2 cups chicken broth and thyme. Scape bottom of pan and continue boiling until creamy. If sauce gets to thick add a little water or more broth. Strain and serve with turkey. Enjoy!

Buttermilk Fried Chicken with Yellow Tomatoes. Kiwi. Watermelon and Feta Vinaigrette

Serves 6 to 8 | Prep Time 30 minutes | Cook Time 15 minutes

WHY I LOVE THIS RECIPE: Buttermilk Fried Chicken is so versatile. The batter in this recipe can be used for any vegetable, fish, chicken or meat. The batter freezes easily and can be stored in small containers. By combining this delicious feta dressing as a dipping sauce for the fruits and chicken, you have a very well rounded satisfying meal. The colors and flavors are wonderful. Remember, we first eat with our eyes. Enjoy! I also use this recipe for my buttermilk pancakes.

INGREDIENTS YOU'LL NEED

3 to 4 boneless, skinless chicken thighs (each thigh cut into 1 inch pieces)
1/2 tablespoon dry mustard
2 teaspoons paprika
6 garlic cloves minced
2 tablespoons flour
Sea salt to taste
2 cups canola oil
* * *
Buttermilk Batter:
1 egg
1 tablespoon canola oil
1 tablespoon agave
2 teaspoons lemon juice
1 teaspoon baking powder
1/2 cup flour
1 cup buttermilk or Greek yogurt
* * *
Feta Vinaigrette – (see Sauces, Stocks, and Vinaigrettes)
* * *
Garnish
6 to 8 1 inch squares watermelon, kiwi and yellow tomato
1 tablespoon chive oil
1/4 cup watercress leaves

DIRECTIONS

Place chicken thigh cubes in bowl and season with dry mustard, paprika, garlic and flour. Cover and refrigerate for 1 hour.

To make buttermilk batter, mix egg, oil, agave, and lemon juice. Whisk in baking powder, then flour. Whisk in buttermilk or yogurt. Let sit overnight.

Make Feta Vinaigrette accordingly. Heat oil in large saucepan to 375º 30 minutes before serving.

When ready to serve, Arrange watermelon, kiwi and tomato on plate. Dip chicken into batter and drop into hot oil. Cook until golden brown. Drain on paper towels to absorb excess oil. Do two times separate paper towels. Season with sea salt. Place on plate and dot with Feta Vinaigrette and chive oil. Garnish with watercress. Serve and enjoy!

Chicken with Mushroom Crust, Glazed Baby Onions, Mushroom Sauce and Laced Potato Chips

Serves 6 | Prep Time | Cook Time

WHY I LOVE THIS RECIPE: This is a great recipe to make ahead of time and just bake at the last minute. The presentation is so beautiful and the taste is heavenly. When truffles are in season , you can add some to the crust and substitute the olive oil for some white truffle oil.

INGREDIENTS YOU'LL NEED

Baby Onion and Porcini Mushroom Sauce – this may be made in advance and frozen:
2 tablespoons olive oil
18 baby onions peeled
5 garlic cloves minced
1 cup Chicken Stock (see Sauces, Stocks, and Vinaigrettes)

* * *

12 Porcini white mushrooms diced
¼ cup Madeira wine
1½ cups Browned Beef Stock (see Sauces, Stocks, and Vinaigrettes)
Sea salt to taste
Pepper to taste
6 tablespoons sweet butter

* * *

Chicken:
6 chicken breasts, halves, save tenderloin
Sea salt to taste
Pepper to taste
Olive Oil

* * *

Mushroom Crust:
1½ pounds shitake mushrooms, diced
½ pound white mushrooms diced
5 shallots, diced
3 large garlic gloves, minced

* * *

Potato Chips:
1 potato thinly sliced
1 cup canola oil

* * *

Garlic Mashed Potatoes:
2 Yukon gold potatoes peeled and cut into 8 pieces
4 garlic cloves, peeled and blanched 3 times in boiling water
½ cup cream
1 stick sweet butter, room temperature
½ teaspoon sea salt

DIRECTIONS

For Baby Onion and Porcini Mushroom Sauce, heat 1 tablespoon olive oil and add baby onions. Sauté until golden brown. Add garlic and Chicken Stock that you already made. Cook until it is reduced by half.

Add 1 tablespoon remaining olive oil to skillet. Add mushrooms and sauté until golden brown. Deglaze pan with Madeira wine and Browned Chicken Stock that you already made. Reduce until lightly thickened. Mix with onions. Season with salt and pepper. Store in jar in refrigerator until ready to use. Just before serving, swirl in butter.

Season chicken breast with sea salt, pepper, garlic, and a little olive oil.

For Mushroom Crust, place diced shiitake mushrooms, white mushrooms, and shallots in large non-stick skillet. Sauté until all liquid is absorbed and mushrooms are golden brown. Remove to food processor with chicken tenderloin and puree. Season with sea salt and pepper.

Coat six pieces of plastic wrap with a little olive oil. Thinly spread mixture over each piece of plastic wrap. Cover with another piece of plastic wrap by overlapping one piece on top, patting down thinly. Lift off plastic wrap and place chicken breast on mushroom crust. Carefully lift plastic wrap and place topping over. Twist ends and refrigerate until ready to serve.

Add 1 tablespoon remaining olive oil to skillet; add mushrooms and sauté until golden brown. Deglaze pan with Madeira wine and Browned Chicken Stock. Reduce until lightly thickened. Mix with onions.

When ready to serve heat oven to 450º. Remove chicken from plastic wrap and place on cookie sheet lined with parchment. Bake 10-11 minutes. Cool about 5 minutes. Slice.

For Potato Chips, heat canola and fry potatoes until golden. **I used a spiralizer for the potatoes on the top, but you can simply use the fried potato chips

For Garlic Mashed Potatoes, place potatoes in saucepan and cover with 2 inches of water. Bring to boil. Reduce heat and cover and cook 30 minutes or until potatoes are tender. Place garlic cloves in garlic press. Place garlic into the heavy cream and cook 3 minutes to blend. Drain water from potatoes. Cover pan and let steam 5 minutes. Mash potatoes with masher. Add sweet butter and garlic cream. Season with sea salt and strain potatoes to remove lumps; set aside.

Heat reserved Onion Mushroom Sauce and swirl in butter one piece at a time. Season with salt and pepper. Place chicken on plate, garnish with Sauce, Potato Chips and Mashed Potatoes. Serve and enjoy!

Grilled Seasoned Tenderloin of Lamb on Purple Yam Tempura. Sake Glaze. Carrots And White Asparagus

Serves 6 to 8 servings | Prep Time 30 minutes | Cook Time

WHY I LOVE THIS RECIPE: This is a wonderful, delicious and colorful recipe to recipe to prepare. The lamb tenderloins are ideal for marinating overnight. The sake glaze which I find will stay for such a long period of time in the refrigerator. This makes life so easy. Prepare when you have extra time. The only thing last minute is grilling the lamb tenderloin and making the tempura batter. Fry the potatoes to a very pleasing crunch. Place on plate garnish with sake glaze. It does not get better. Our step brother Randy Gingold loved steak. It was the first dinner we made for him when we came to our house. He will live in our hearts with love forever. Enjoy!

INGREDIENTS YOU'LL NEED

SEASONINGS
Himalayan Sea Salt
Paprika
2 garlic cloves crushed
2 teaspoons fresh ginger, peeled and grated
2 teaspoons dry English mustard
2 tablespoons maple syrup
2 tablespoons mushroom soy
1 tablespoon sesame oil
3 tablespoons extra virgin olive oil

PURPLE YAMS
1 large purple yam cooked, peel removed and cut into 1 ½ inch rounds 2 inches high
2 pound tenderloin of lamb

SAKE GLAZE
¼ cup mushroom soy
¼ cup rice wine vinegar
⅛ cup sake
1 tablespoon fresh lime juice
1 tablespoon grated maui onion
⅛ cup sesame oil
1 tablespoon fresh minced garlic
11/2 tablespoon fresh
Ginger to taste
2 tables fresh Maple syrup

GARNISH
12 to 16 sliced cooked carrots, optional
6 to 8 white peeled asparagus, optional
Fried spinach leaves

DIRECTIONS

Season lamb tenderloin with all the seasonings.Reserve in refrigerator until ready to grill.Combine all the ingredients for sake glaze and refrigerate. Place purple yams in a warm oven. Heat olive oil over a very hot grill. Grill lamb tenderloin and cook until very brown on all sides. Keep warm in 250 degree oven with yams. Heat olive oil in a non-stick skillet. Add vegetables and when they are brown, add the smoked brown sugar and cook until sugar dissolves. Season yams with kosher salt. Slice tenderloin into 1 ½ inch pieces and place one piece on a purple yam slice .Place on plate . Garnish with carrots, asparagus and sake glaze. Enjoy! Dill Vinaigrette is excellent with this too.

PAIRS WELL WITH: Merlot

Grilled Tomahawk Steak

Serves 6 tob 8 | Prep Time 10 minutes | Cook Time 20 minutes

WHY I LOVE THIS RECIPE: This recipe is a favorite of Chris Reed. This is what Chris Reed wrote. " I have 6 children. My oldest is 57 and he and his family have a particular passion for steaks. We share tomahawks about twice a year. Always a special occasion".

INGREDIENTS YOU'LL NEED

2 -2 inch Tomahawk Steaks, grass fed and organic if possible
**Can be purchased at Kroger markets, or an organic market.
3 teaspoons kosher salt
1 teaspoon freshly ground black pepper
extra virgin olive oil
Whiskey smoked brown sugar or plain brown sugar ** smoked sugar can be purchased online from DarkHorse specialty foods

DIRECTIONS

At least 1 hour before you plan to grill the steaks, season with kosher salt and freshly ground pepper. This may even be done the night before. Cover the steaks with plastic wrap and refrigerate. Remove the steaks from the refrigerator when you preheat the grill. Set the grill on the highest temperature possible. First grill steaks with the bone and back side on the grill. Close lid and cook for 5 to 10 minutes. Flip the steaks so that the bone is now up . Cook about 2 minutes on each angle. Turn over and grill the other side. Sprinkle with brown sugar and grill 30 minutes on both sides or until browned and crusty but not burned. Move to a large platter and let rest for 10 minutes. Show the steaks to your guests. Put the steaks on a cutting board and run a sharp knife along the curve of the bone to carve the meat in 1/2 inch slices. Serve on a presentation platter. Enjoy

PAIRS WELL WITH: Cabernet Sauvignon

Pat Cairns. Old Ladies on a Bus Chicken with Barbecue Sauce

Serves Makes 4 1/2 cups | Prep Time 10 minutes | Cook Time 30 to 45 minutes

WHY I LOVE THIS RECIPE: "I have worked in Malibu schools since 1973 in September of 1988 we moved to Malibu West, and over the years, we have packed and unpacked many times as fire approached our area. It was in the early morning of November 9,2018, when we had to evacuate as a " Here is my story and the easiest recipe I have! I didn't say this in my story, but about 5 years ago I collected recipes from my sisters and nieces and asked for handwritten recipes that my mother had sent them as well as their own. One sister and I had collected and printed them up in little binders for all of us. My copy "Died" in the fire, but one of my sisters had an extra copy of the book which she gave me this summer. The Old Ladies on a Bus is one of the recipes in that family cookbook. Had we not done that as a project, all of my mother's handwritten recipes would have been lost. It turned out, I had the greatest number of the recipes. They are a history of my family, and I am so thrilled we still have them. We now add to that family cookbook but not as often as we should

INGREDIENTS YOU'LL NEED

2 cups Homemade Barbeque Sauce (see Sauces, Stocks, and Vinaigrettes) OR your favorite store-bought sauce
1 cup orange/lemon marmalade
juice of 1/2 -1 lemon
a bit of Worcestershire sauce (to taste), honestly I always forget to add this
8 chicken breast or thigh pieces (I use breasts because that is what we like)

DIRECTIONS

Combine barbeque sauce, marmalade, lemon juice, and Worcestershire sauce. Place chicken pieces in a baking dish; cover with sauce mixture and bake at 350 degrees until done. 30 to 45 minutes. May be sliced and placed on plate. Enjoy.

Pat says, "I never measure any of this. I just make enough sauce to top the chicken but drown it in the sauce. When it is all cooked, I reduce the sauce in a small pan until it is a little thicker to put on the chicken and rice. I serve it with wild rice, a green vegetable, and salad and sometimes if I have it on hand, I heat up buttered French bread to go along with it. I use leftovers sliced on top of salad for the next day."

PAIRS WELL WITH: chardonnay or Champagne or Beer

Poached Sea Scallops with Lemon ,Cauliflower, Horseradish and Sesame Chili Pepper Chips

Serves 6 | Prep Time | Cook Time

WHY I LOVE THIS RECIPE: This recipe is filled with wonderful and different flavors and colors to delight the eye and your taste buds. The horseradish and lemon sauce is just perfect for the scallops which are very lightly poached.

Grated fresh cauliflower and chili chips are quite a surprise.

INGREDIENTS YOU'LL NEED

Poached Sea Scallops:
6 large fresh sea scallops
Sea salt to taste
Freshly ground pepper to taste
* * *
Sesame chili red pepper chips:
1/3 cup red pepper
1 tablespoon agave
1 tablespoon black sesame seeds
Sea salt to taste
* * *
1 tablespoon lemon peel, grated
1 lemon, sectioned out
2 tablespoons agave
1 tablespoon cut chives
* * *
Sauce:
½ cup Homemade Mayonnaise – (see Sauces, Stocks, and Vinaigrettes)
½ cup plain Icelandic siggi's yogurt
2 tablespoons horseradish
½ cup cauliflower, pureed
¼ cup fresh cauliflower
Sea salt to taste

DIRECTIONS

For the scallops, bring a large pan of water to boil. Add scallops. Reduce heat and cover pan. Simmer for 3 to 5 minutes.

For sesame chips, puree red pepper with agave and a little water. Spread on silpat and sprinkle with sesame seeds. Season with sea salt. Dehydrate for 10 hours. Turn over and dehydrate by placing in 135 degree oven for 8 hours more. Place lemon sections in 2 tablespoons agave.

To make sauce, combine all ingredients, except grated cauliflower, in medium bowl. Strain and set aside.

Place sauce on plate. Arrange scallops, grated cauliflower, lemon peel, lemon sections, chives and chips around plate. Serve and enjoy!

Prime Filet and Braised Short Ribs with Green Beans

Serves 8 | Prep Time 35 minutes | Cook Time 7 hours

WHY I LOVE THIS RECIPE: Pairing Filet Mignon with Short Ribs is one of my all time favorites. When you are finished cooking the short Ribs, you will have the most fantastic stock. I strain and chill the stock. The next day, I remove all the fat and place the stock in a large saucepan and add about 12 cloves of peeled garlic and 5 sprigs of thyme. I then turn the heat up and let the stock reduce by 2/3rds . It can be frozen at this point and used whenever you need. This is the way to go! To make the presentation a little nicer, after I slice the fillet, I place it on the short rib bone and place some short ribs next to it. It is then sauced and served. Wow!

INGREDIENTS YOU'LL NEED

Eight 3 bone short ribs cut 1" thick by 4" long
Four 4 ounce prime filet mignon steaks, seasoned with sea salt, pepper, olive oil
Sea salt to taste
Freshly ground pepper to taste
Dry mustard
Paprika
Flour
1/3 cup olive oil
1 red onion, chopped
4 cloves garlic, whole, unpeeled
3 cloves garlic, peeled, minced
1 leek, chopped
1 carrot, peeled, chopped

2 tablespoons olive oil
2 tablespoons butter
* * *
½ cup heavy cream
5 garlic cloves
⅓ chicken broth
* * *
2 tablespoons olive oil
1 red onion
1/4 good quality port wine
5 cloves minced fresh garlic
2 cups cooked green beans
1 cup reserved beef broth

DIRECTIONS

Season short ribs with sea salt, pepper, dry mustard, paprika, and flour. Heat 1/3 cup olive oil in a large skillet; brown short ribs on all sides. Remove short ribs from skillet and place in roasting pan. In the skillet where ribs were browned, sauté vegetables and cook until very brown. Remove from skillet and add the vegetables to the roasting pan where the meat is now.

Add water to skillet to where meat and vegetables were cooked in. Bring to boil; pour water over short ribs to cover. Cover with tin foil. Bake 350 degrees for 2 hours. Reduce heat to 275 degrees and bake 3 hours more. Strain and place broth in refrigerator. Chill overnight and remove the fat. Reduce to 1 cup with minced garlic. Strain.

For, garlic cream sauce, mix garlic with cream and reduce slowly until lightly thick. Add chicken broth and reduce until thick. Strain and reserve.

When ready to serve, heat medium skillet with 2 tablespoons olive oil. When hot, sauté fillet mignon until very brown on all sides, cook about 8 minutes. Remove to plate and keep warm. Add remaining onions to skillet and sauté until very brown. Deglaze pan with port. Add reduced reserved broth. Reduce until slightly thickened, stir in butter and keep warm. Slice fillet 1/8" thick. Heat short ribs until hot. Remove thin layer of fat that attached short rib to bone and place short rib on half on the bone. Place slices of steak on other half of bone. Place cooked green beans on plate and place short rib and steak on green beans. Pour wine sauce around fillet mignon and garlic sauce in between. Serve. Enjoy!

Life isn't about
finding
yourself.....it's about
creating yourself

Melanie's Shepard's Pie

Serves 8 to 10 servings | Prep Time 45 minutes | Cook Time 15 minutes

WHY I LOVE THIS RECIPE: This is traditional British comfort food, perfect for cooler nights, and easy to prepare ahead of time for a fast, nourishing dinner after work or school activities.

INGREDIENTS YOU'LL NEED

3 to 4 tablespoons olive oil or oil of your choice 1 large onion chopped
1 1/2 to 2 pounds ground beef, chicken, turkey, veal or lamb 2 cups beef broth
4 tablespoons flour
5 to 6 large Yukon potatoes
1 cup milk, 1/2 and 1/2 or cream 1 tsp. Sea salt
1 stick sweet butter

DIRECTIONS

Preheat oven to 425 degrees. This recipe maybe assembled and finished in the oven later when needed. Heat the 3 tablespoons of the oil in a skillet and fry the onions until soft and beginning to brown. At the same time in another skillet fry the meat until almost cooked.. Drain the fat and add to the onions. When is the onion is softened but not to brown , add the flour and stir for a few moments to cook the flour taste. Lower the heat and off the heat add the beef broth and stir to combine. Return to heat and bring to a boil stirring g constantly until thick and smooth. Season with salt to taste and pepper. Then add the meat and stir to combine. Remove from heat and pour into a baking dish so that the it comes up the sides by 2/3. Reserve.

Peel and chop the potatoes, add to the boiling water and cook until soft. This will take about 30 minutes. Drain . Mash potatoes with a potato masher. Mash in butter and milk , a little at a time. You want this free of lumps. You may spoon the mashed potatoes on top or they may be placed in a piping bag and piped over the meat. Bake in preheated oven for 10 to 15 minutes or until golden brown on top.

Tips and variations:

- Add peas, sweet corn, carrots, or beans chopped to the mixture.
- Try adding Worcestershire sauce to the meat.
- You may add grated cheeses on top of the potatoes before placing in oven.
- You may freeze this recipe unbaked.

SHEMESHFARMS
MALIBU RAW
SHEMESHFARMS
HAND PICKED BY SHEMESH FARM FELLOWS
SALT N ROSES
CREATED WITH SOUL IN MALIBU

Swordfish with Shemesh Farms Seasoning and Honey

Serves 4 to 6 servings | Prep Time 10 minutes | Cook Time 15 minutes

WHY I LOVE THIS RECIPE: When I saw the offering of salts with herbs at the Shemesh farms, I went to work thinking about a great recipe with these amazing seasonings. I came up with this recipe which was delicious with the swordfish. They have the last of the Malibu Honey that was rescued from the fire. It is so special and delicious. Michele is a gift and blessing to this world. She gives jobs to kids with special needs and actually pays them. Their farm was burnt down during the Woolsey Fire. The owner, Michelle Cait only employs and pays young adults with special needs to help harvest their products. You can buy their products online at Shemeshfarms.com.

INGREDIENTS YOU'LL NEED

4 to 6 pieces, 4 ounce swordfish steaks
3 tablespoons extra virgin olive oil
Shemesh farms , Salt N Roses to taste
freshly ground white pepper
2 tablespoons raw honey
4 to 6 tablespoons dijon mustard

DIRECTIONS

Heat grill too high. Season swordfish with Salt N Roses and freshly ground white pepper. When ready to serve. Place swordfish on grill and cook 3 minutes. Turn slightly to crisscross lines on grill . Cook 3 to 5 minutes more. Turn over completely and repeat grilling. Brush each plate with dijon mustard and drizzly with a little honey, Cut swordfish in half and place 1//2 on each plate. Lean the other half on side. Maybe served with any vegetable or starch. Enjoy

PAIRS WELL WITH: Chardonnay or Champagne or Beer

...she knew the sea, had her back.

Desserts

Cheesecake Lollipops

Serves 15 | Prep Time | Cook Time

WHY I LOVE THIS RECIPE: There are times when just a taste of something is all you crave. This is how I came up with this recipe. When I am entertaining, I never want my guests to go home hungry. Sometimes I make a few different desserts but I want to make the last bite memorable. This is when the cheesecake lollipops are perfect. I let them stay at room temperature about 30 minutes or more before serving. The lollipops will be creamy and delicious.

INGREDIENTS YOU'LL NEED

1 8 ounce package cream cheese, softened
¼ cup baker's sugar
2 teaspoons vanilla
½ teaspoon vanilla bean paste
* * *
8 ounces white chocolate, melted
4 ounces dark chocolate, melted
4 ounces milk chocolate, melted
½ cup warm caramel
1/3 cup almonds, macadamia nuts or pumpkin seeds, chopped
15 lollipop sticks

DIRECTIONS

In a bowl, combine cream cheese, sugar, vanilla, and vanilla bean paste until creamy. Place bowl in freezer until firm, about an hour. With small melon baller, roll out 15 balls and place on cookie sheet lined with wax paper. Stick a stick through center of lollipop and refreeze until hard.

Dip all the lollipops in white chocolate and refrigerate.

Dip 5 to of the lollipops into caramel and nuts.

Dip 5 of the lollipops that were dipped into the white chocolate and half into the dark chocolate to make a tuxedo.

Dip 5 of the lollipops halfway into milk chocolate. Refrigerate until ready to serve. Enjoy!

Chocolate Baby Grand Piano Filled with English Toffee

Serves 6 | Prep Time 30 minutes | Cook Time 6 minutes for toffee

WHY I LOVE THIS RECIPE: I love bringing this out for dessert when I have company over. It's elegant and decadent. The chocolate piano melts in your mouth and the english toffee is nothing like you've ever tasted. The best part about making this dessert is knowing that you can always save some extra toffee for yourself :)

INGREDIENTS YOU'LL NEED

Piano mold - can be purchased online at lifeoftheparty.com, along with Wilton candy melts chocolate.
48 ounces milk chocolate, semi-sweet chocolate or white chocolate, melted
1 ounce milk chocolate or white chocolate, melted
* * *
English Toffee:
1 cup sugar
2 sticks sweet butter
¼ cup water
Pinch salt
1½ teaspoons vanilla
* * *
12 ounces milk chocolate
½ cup roasted almonds, finely diced

DIRECTIONS

To make piano, fill each mold piece with 8 ounces of the chocolate of your choice. Chill and unmold. Assemble piano and paint piano keys with opposite color chocolate. Fill inside of piano with English toffee. Repeat to make a total of 6 pianos.

For English Toffee, butter 9"x 13" nonstick baking sheet. Combine sugar, butter, water, and salt in saucepan. Place over medium-high heat and bring to a strong boil, stirring until sugar dissolves. Continue boiling until mixture becomes syrupy and golden brown. Remove from heat and stir in vanilla. Pour into prepared baking sheet. Cool and let harden.

Melt chocolate. Lift toffee from baking sheet and spread half of the chocolate over. Sprinkle with almonds. Place in refrigerator one hour or until it hardens. Turn over and quickly spread other side with chocolate. Sprinkle remaining almonds over. Refrigerate again until hard. Break into desired shapes. If serving with cake, arrange over cake. Serve and enjoy!

Chocolate Cherry Truffles

Serves Makes 18 truffles | Prep Time | Cook Time

WHY I LOVE THIS RECIPE: The perfect bite sized truffle to have around the house or to take wrapped nicely for a dinner party. These truffles are seemingly easy to make and give a little extra kick for any holiday treat or just because you deserve it!

INGREDIENTS YOU'LL NEED

12 ounces good quality milk chocolate

* * *

½ cup heavy cream
1 cup water
2 tablespoons cherry Brandy

* * *

Butter for lining pan
½ cup sugar
¼ cup water
2 tablespoons Kirsch
18 cherries with stems

* * *

Good quality cocoa

* * *

10 ounces good quality semi-sweet chocolate, melted

DIRECTIONS

Place 12 ounces chocolate into ovenproof bowl. Place in 200 degrees oven for 10 minutes. Remove from oven and stir. Chocolate will be lumpy. Return to oven for 10 minutes more. Remove and stir until smooth.

Combine sugar and water in a small saucepan, stirring until smooth. Bring to boil over high heat. Cool and add Kirsch. Place syrup in bowl and add cherries. Marinate 1 week or more.
Cook and stir 10 minutes more. Remove from heat. Cool 5 minutes. Spread quickly in a buttered 8 inch square pan. Chill overnight and reserve.

Heat cream in double boiler over 1 cup of boiling water. When bubbles appear, remove from heat. Gradually pour the cream into the melted chocolate, beating with a wooden spoon until combined, dark and shiny. Return chocolate mixture to double boiler. Cook over medium heat over boiling water, stirring constantly for 15 minutes. Add 2 Tbl. cherry b randy. Cook and stir 10. minutes more. Remove from heat. Cool 5 minutes. Spread quickly in a buttered 8 inch square pan. Chill overnight and reserve.

Take a teaspoon of truffle and pat into flat pancake. Place one cherry in center and enclose truffle around cherry. Refrigerate. Continue with remaining truffle and cherries. Roll in cocoa. Enjoy at room temperature.

White Chocolate Peanut Butter Cups

Serves Makes 60 cups | Prep Time 35. minutes | Cook Time no cooking in this recipes, just melting chocolate

WHY I LOVE THIS RECIPE: These candies are so much fun to make together with someone. The delicious peanut butter stuffed inside the white chocolate is heavenly. If you prefer, you could do the same recipe with dark or milk chocolate. We each have our favorites. Enjoy.

INGREDIENTS YOU'LL NEED

½ cup creamy peanut butter
½ cup powdered sugar
1 tablespoon softened butter
1 teaspoon vanilla
* * *
12 ounces chocolate (white, dark or carob chips), melted
* * *
Small candy cups

DIRECTIONS

Combine peanut butter, sugar, butter and vanilla. Chill. Roll into small balls and refrigerate.

Drip clean paint brush into melted chocolate. Paint inside of paper cup with chocolate, making sure to go up the sides. Chill until firm on cookie sheet.

Place one small ball of peanut butter mixture into candy cup. Place one teaspoon of chocolate over peanut butter to cover. Chill until chocolate is firm. Serve and enjoy!

PAIRS WELL WITH: Kaluha and cream

Christmas Carrot Cake Compliments of Lisa McKean

Serves 12 servings | Prep Time 20 minutes | Cook Time 40 minutes

WHY I LOVE THIS RECIPE: A delicious carrot cake even Bugs Bunny would approve of! So light and fluffy!

INGREDIENTS YOU'LL NEED

Cake
2 cups whole wheat or gluten free flour
2 cups dark brown sugar
1 tablespoon cinnamon
1 tablespoon ginger
1/4 teaspoon cloves
1/4 tsp. nutmeg
1 tablespoon baking powder

1 1/3 cup sunflower or canola oil
5 large eggs, room temperature

2 heaping cups grated fresh organic carrots
1 cup raisons
1 cup walnuts

Frosting
8 ounces cream cheese room temperature
8 ounces sweet butter , room temperature
12 ounces or more powdered sugar

oil to grease pans
1/2 cup crushed nuts of choice

DIRECTIONS

Blend all the dry ingredients thoroughly in a large bowl. In a smaller bowl, whisk together the oil and eggs until creamy and blended. Add the grated carrots, raisons and nuts of your choice. Stir mixture until well combined, then stir in dry ingredients. Pour into a greased floured and parchment lined 9

x13 inch pan or 3 , 7- inch round cake pans. Bake 40 t0 45 minutes or until knife inserted comes out clean. Cool 12 minutes on rack and turn over. When completely cool frost.

For frosting , cream butter and sugar together in a large mixing bowl. Gradually beat in sugar. Beat until light and fluffy. Add more sugar for a stiffer frosting.Sprinkle with a handful of nuts. Enjoy.

PAIRS WELL WITH: Hot Chocolate or a cup of tea

MALIBU

Dr. Lisa's Jalapeno Cornbread Cupcakes with Honey Buttercream

Makes 25 to 30 cupcakes | Prep Time 30 minutes | Cook Time 15 to 18 minutes

WHY I LOVE THIS RECIPE: "These cupcakes are filled with flavor and spice. A different twist for a great treat!" Dr. Lisa, from Malibu Coast Animal Hospital, just donated 500 of her delicious treats to One Love Malibu Concert, which Katy Perry attended. Dr. Lisa's heart is so big and according to her husband, 50 hours working is not enough. Thanks Dr. Lisa for your beautiful and generous spirit. These cupcakes are fun to make and the surprise is the bite from the jalapeños. (The editor grated a little chocolate on the top. This is optional but very good!)

INGREDIENTS YOU'LL NEED

Cupcakes
2 2//3 cups all-purpose flour
2/3 cup yellow cornmeal
1 teaspoon baking powder
1/2 teaspoon baking soda
1/2 teaspoon salt
1 cup softened sweet butter
1 cup raw honey
1 cup sugar
1 cup milk
1/2 cup sour cream
4 eggs
1 teaspoon vanilla
1 seeded and finely chopped jalapenos

Icing
1 cup sweet butter room temperature
4 cups powdered sugar
1/2 cup raw honey
1/2 cup cold sour cream

DIRECTIONS

For cupcakes, Preheat oven to 350 degrees and line muffin tins with cupcake liners. In a medium bowl, combine flour, cornmeal, baking powder, baking soda and salt. Set aside. In a large mixing bowl, use electric mixer (hand or standing) to beat butter, honey and sugar together until light and fluffy (2 minutes) Beat in eggs one at a time. Add all the liquid ingredients along with half of the dry ingredients and mix until well combined. Fold in the jalapeños. Fill tins 2/3 full (25-30 regular sized cupcakes) and bake for 15 to 18 minutes. or until a toothpick comes out clean. (start making frosting while cupcakes are cooking). Cool for 5 minutes in tins and then remove onto a wire rack to cool completely. Chill frosting 30 minutes. Spread on cupcake or pipe through a pastry bag. Just eat them as is because they are delicious. For frosting: In a medium sized mixing bowl, beat butter for three minutes with a electric mixer on high speed until light and fluffy. Mix in powered sugar a little at a time until full combined. Mix in honey and sour cream until combined. Spread or pipe. onto cooled cupcakes.

PAIRS WELL WITH: Coffee or a Vanilla Malt

French Macaroons

Serves Makes 20 in each color | Prep Time | Cook Time

WHY I LOVE THIS RECIPE: Just being able to make your own French macaroons is such a great feeling. These are the delicious cookies you find in most bakeries in Paris, New York and Los Angeles. You are bringing these places to your own home and feeling pretty wonderful about your accomplishments. Go ahead, have some fun! **Do n to make these on a damp day, or your cookies won't get crunchy...but will remain soggy.

INGREDIENTS YOU'LL NEED

2½ cups almond flour
2 cups plus 2 tablespoons confectioners' sugar
1 cup granulated sugar
1/3 cup water
15 tablespoons liquid egg whites, room temperature
5 assorted pastel food coloring
* * *

Filling:
2 large eggs
¾ cup sugar
¼ cup water
1 teaspoon vanilla
Dash salt
Food coloring
1/8 pound very cold sweet butter

DIRECTIONS

Preheat oven to 350 degrees. Line baking sheets with parchment paper. You may place parchment paper directly on counter to pipe out.

To make the meringue for the cookies, In a food processor, pulse the almond and confectioners' sugar. Sift with a fine mesh strainer. Divide mixture into 5 small bowls.

In a small saucepan, combine granulated sugar and 1/3 cup water. Stir and bring to boil. Cook 5 minutes. Place 9 tablespoons egg whites in mixer. Beat until foamy and thick. Gradually add hot sugar syrup and beat until cool.

Divide remaining egg whites in 5 small cups and generously add food coloring. Mix each color egg white into almond mixture. Place cooled meringue into each color, half the amount at a time. Transfer to disposable piping bags and pipe to small circle on parchment paper. Let dry 10 to 20 minutes or longer. Bake 350 degrees for 8 to 10 minutes.

For Filling, whisk all ingredients together, except butter; bring to boil. Whisk continuously for 10 minutes. Remove from heat. Stir in butter and cool. Divide into 5 small cups and color the same as the macaroons. Spread on one macaroon and make a sandwich in same color. Continue with different colors until all are filled. Serve and enjoy!

BLUE
BROWN
GRAY

Grandma Abrams filled Strawberry Jam Hazelnut Cookies

Serves Makes 2 dozen cookies | Prep Time | Cook Time

WHY I LOVE THIS RECIPE: My grandmother was the true baker and mentor for me with cooking from scratch. My mother was an amazing artist with food and could take a chunk of ice and crave it into something beautiful. My grandmother on the other time loved to cook. She just knew what tasted right. I remember when I would go to her house when I was first married to my husband for cooking lessons and I would say to her , "please measure Grandma". She smiled and said just feel what you need. Now I see what she means. When I first started , that was not the case and I liked everything measured. Have fun cooking it is a gift form your heart!

INGREDIENTS YOU'LL NEED

1 cup sweet butter, softened
1 cup powdered sugar
1 tablespoon brandy or rum
1 cup ground hazelnuts
2 cups flour, sifted
½ teaspoon baking powder
* * *
½ cup Strawberry jam- this makes 2 cups, but you can use
remaining jam for another time:
2 cups sugar
2 cups water
6 cups beautifully ripe strawberries
* * *
Powdered sugar

DIRECTIONS

Cream butter and powdered sugar until fluffy. Add brandy, hazelnuts, baking powder, and flour. Blend until dough is soft. Place in plastic wrap or baggie and refrigerate overnight. Roll out half of the dough between 2 pieces of plastic wrap on top a cold board and cut with 1½-inch fluted cookie cutter. Cut small circles in center of half of the cookies. Place on parchment-lined cookie sheet and bake at 350 degrees for 12 to 15 minutes. Cool on cookie rack.

For Strawberry Jam, bring sugar and water to boil over high heat. Boil until sugar dissolves in water. Let cool. Slice green leaves and stems of strawberries off and discard. Place strawberries into large bowl. Pour sugar/water mixture over top and cover tightly with plastic wrap. Marinate for 3 days at room temperature. This will bring the natural pectin out of the fruit. Pour strawberries and liquid into a large 12-inch non-stick pan. Bring mixture to a boil and reduce heat. Simmer until thick. Pour into jars. Cool and cover. Refrigerate. Use as needed.

Spread strawberry jam on bottom of cookie with hole. Sprinkle powdered sugar on cookie with hole. Sandwich together. Fill remaining jam into parchment cone. Pipe into center. Place on plates. Serve and enjoy!

YOUR

Kaluha Coffee Truffles

Serves Makes one dozen truffles | Prep Time 30 minutes | Cook Time 30 minutes

WHY I LOVE THIS RECIPE: “This would be a great gift for for any party. Just make sure to have enough.” Kahlua truffles are my favorite. They are always part of my Christmas candy box, They are easy to make ahead and they keep for months in the refrigerator. Just make sure to take them out 1 hour before you plan to serve. Enjoy these creamy delights.

INGREDIENTS YOU'LL NEED

12 ounces good quality chocolate

* * *

¾ cup heavy cream

2 teaspoons instant coffee

2 tablespoons Kahlua

24 candy coffee beans

8 ounces good quality chocolate for dipping. Use Wiltons candy melts in dark. chocolate (you can purchase at Michaels or on line at lifeoftheparty.com)

DIRECTIONS

Shred 12 ounces chocolate in food processor. Place chocolate in ovenproof bowl. Place in warm 175 degrees oven for 10 minutes. Stir and let remain in oven until melted.

Heat heavy cream in top of double boiler until cream is bubbling steadily. Add 2 teaspoons instant coffee. Gradually pour coffee cream into melted chocolate. Beat with spoon until dark and shiny. Return chocolate coffee mixture to double boiler. Cook over boiling water, stirring constantly for 15 minutes. Add 2 tablespoons Kahlua Cook and stir 10 minutes more. Remove mixture from heat. Cool 5 minutes. Spread quickly into a buttered 8-inch square pan. Chill until firm. Take a spoonful out and flatten it in your hands. Place one candy coffee bean in center. Enclose candy bean with a truffle. Refrigerate.

Shred remaining 8 ounces of chocolate in food processor. Melt as described for 12 ounces chocolate. Cool chocolate to room temperature. Dip each chocolate truffle in chocolate. Place one candy coffee bean on top. Place on tray lined with waxed paper. . Refrigerate. Serve and enjoy!

PAIRS WELL WITH: Caramel Martini

Chocolate Caramel Turtles by Edie Rogers

Serves Makes 24 to 30 turtles | Prep Time 35 minutes | Cook Time 15 minutes

WHY I LOVE THIS RECIPE: "I talked to my mother-in-law Edie every day and we always discussed wonderful recipes. This was one of her favorite. She was a wonderful treasure!" Caramel is wonderful to have in your refrigerator at all times. It is the most fabulous topping for almost anything. These turtles are a must for the holidays. I always include them in my homemade chocolates to family and friends. You will love them!

INGREDIENTS YOU'LL NEED

Vanilla Caramel: 2½ cups sugar
1 cup plus 3 tablespoons water
¼ cup Cream of Tartar
1/3 cup whipping cream, room temperature
1 stick butter
2/3 stick vanilla
* * *
12 ounces milk chocolate, Wiltons ca nay coating or Lindt chocolate 1 pound pecans or raw toasted cashews

DIRECTIONS

For Vanilla Caramel, combine sugar, water, and cream of tartar. Stir until mixture comes to a boil. When mixture becomes a dark caramel color, stop stirring. Remove mixture from heat and cool 15 seconds. Pour in whipping cream and swirl to mix. Let butter melt over top. Stir when butter melts. Add vanilla. Pour into bowl and place over bowl of ice. Stir until mixture becomes firm. Take about ½ teaspoon of caramel and roll into ball. Place on a silpat lined cookie sheet. Refrigerate.

Spoon chocolate over caramel and leave some nuts showing. Refrigerate. Turn over and coat other side. Refrigerate until chocolate is set. Store at room temperature. Serve and enjoy!

PAIRS WELL WITH: Apple Brandy

Pavlova from Jill Palethorpe

Serves 4 to 6 servings | Prep Time 20 minutes | Cook Time 3 hours

WHY I LOVE THIS RECIPE: "It will be a while before I bake this again (no oven), but even before it was only seen at Easter and Christmas. There is debate about who invented this dessert among the Aussies and Kiwis, but we Aussies win." Our home burned around 11 a.m. on the 9th of November 2018. I left an hour before with my five chickens and rooster, 2 dogs, the horse and the pony in the horse trailer. My husband stayed to fight the fire but even with a proper fire fighting hose and a pump and generators he could not withstand what Mother Nature threw at us that. day. My son tried to get to him to help but could not get in past the roadblock at the bottom of the street. From Paradise Cove , I watched the fire sweep in on all four sides. Around 10 p.m. the fire jumped PCH and ripped into the Cove. I took the horses, chickens and dogs into the water, and we stood in the warm gentle tide while flaming pine cones and palm fronds hit the sand and the shallows all around us. Neighbor's saved the Cove that night with garden hoses and shovels, and I remember feeling strangely reassured as I watched. Maybe it was the calmness of the ponies, the trust of both the dogs at my feet, but I knew we would not burn. I knew we would prevail. Yet we didn't.

INGREDIENTS YOU'LL NEED

Pavlova
4 egg whites
1 1/4 cups baker's sugar
1 Teaspoon white vinegar
1 teaspoon vanilla essence
1 tablespoon corn flour (cornstarch in the States)

Topping

! cup heavy cream whipped with 1/4 cup confectioners sugar and 2 teaspoons vanilla essence
1 large banana sliced
passion fruit
2 kiwis , peeled and sliced
1 cup fresh raspberries
Any fruit of your choice

DIRECTIONS

Preheat the oven to 350 degrees. USE AN ELECTRIC MIXER or your arms will fall off. Beat the egg whites on high for 10 minutes, then drop the speed down and add the sugar slowly. When all the sugar is in, turn the mixer back up to high for 5 minutes.

Digression: Egg whites are the stickiest thing know to man (that's what holds the gold leaf onto illuminated manuscripts) and getting a pavlova off the tray and onto the platter in one piece after it cooks is a challenge. Bake Pavlova on tray lined with parchment. If you want the pavlova to look sort of circular when it's cooked you can draw a 10 inch circle on the parchment lined tray. You may also use a silpat. This can be purchased at specialty cooking stores .

Back to the recipe:
Mix the vinegar, vanilla and corn flour together in a separate bowl. It will be almost unworkable so take a little of the egg white mixture and combine it with the corn flour.

Add the corn flour to the egg whites and beat on high speed for a further 5 minutes.

Turn the mixture out onto the lined baking sheet -allow for a 2-inch creep from the circle you drew or formed.

Put the Pav in the oven , right in the center and immediately lower the oven temp. to 250F. Bake for 1 hour.

DO NOT OPEN THE OVEN DOOR. DO NOT LET ANYONE NEAR THE OVEN WHO CAN'T FLOAT LIKE A BALLERINA.

Turn the oven off and do something else that does''t involve the oven or cooking or even the kitchen for 3 hours.

When the oven is cooled you can open the door

Put the pavlova VERY CAREFULLY onto whatever serving dish you choose and decorate with whipped cream which, thankfully will mask any seismic damage, and fruit (Jill loves bananas and passion fruit-kiwis and raspberries are good too)

Now she says, " You see why I only make this at Easter and Christmas.

Be somebody's rainbow on a cloudy day

Peanut Butter Cheesecake

Serves 6 | Prep Time 15 minutes | Cook Time

WHY I LOVE THIS RECIPE: When I decided I needed something different to impress the Art Museum with a fundraiser dinner, this recipe became one of the deserts. We love cheesecake and I wanted to make something a little different. I decided to add peanut butter to my recipe and then make a little Merry-Go-Round out of cookies for the top of the cake. The top of the tent was out of chocolate. It was a hit and wonderful to eat.

INGREDIENTS YOU'LL NEED

Crust:
1½ cups ground crispy cookie crumbs - chocolate, gingerbread or graham cracker cookies
6 tablespoons butter, melted
2 tablespoons sugar
2 teaspoons cocoa
2 tablespoons peanuts
2 tablespoons peanut butter
3 tablespoons soft butter

* * *

Filling:

8 ounces cream cheese
1 egg yolk
½ cup peanut butter
½ cup sugar
1/2 teaspoon vanilla
½ cup heavy cream, whipped

* * *

Chantilly Cream:
1 cup heavy cream
3 tablespoons sugar
2 teaspoons vanilla extract

* * *

Garnish:
Peanut toffee
Cookies

DIRECTIONS

For Crust, preheat oven to 300 degrees. Combine cookie crumbs, 6 tablespoons butter, sugar, cocoa, and peanuts in work bowl of food processor. Mix until completely blended. Blend in peanut butter. Line 6 ring molds with 3 tablespoons butter. Place rings on parchment paper-lined cookie sheet. Press cookie crumb mixture into 3-inch rings lined with butter. Bake crust 20 to 25 minutes or until golden.

For Filling, beat cream cheese with peanut butter and sugar until light. Add vanilla and fold in heavy cream. Scrape into a small bowl. , stir in the egg yolk and vanilla. Fill center of rings with mixture. Refrigerate overnight.

For Chantilly Cream, whip the heavy cream until light peaks form. Add sugar gradually and vanilla extract. Unmold cheesecake by carefully cutting around rim to loosen crust and release cake. Garnish with cookies, chocolate tent and Chantilly Cream. Serve and enjoy!

Rocky Road in a Chocolate Shoe

Serves Makes 50 pieces | Prep Time 15 minutes | Cook Time Melting chocolate

WHY I LOVE THIS RECIPE: Rocky road is such a easy recipe to make. The great thing about making it is that all the ingredients are mixed together and then placed in a baking dish then placed in the refrigerator until just about set. Do not let the chocolate get to hard before you slice . Depending on what size pan you use to shape the rocky road , it will be either thin or thick. This is up to you. I love putting the leftovers in my homemade vanilla ice cream. You will just love this recipe

INGREDIENTS YOU'LL NEED

Butter for pan
1 teaspoon sweet butter
8 ounces milk chocolate
8 ounces semi-sweet chocolate
1 teaspoon vanilla
20 large marshmallows, quartered or 80 small marshmallows
3½ cups walnuts, chopped

Chocolate Shoe Mold- can be purchased online at lifeoftheparty.com
**all chocolate has to be Wilton candy melt, which can also be purchased at lifeoftheparty.com

6 ounces yellow chocolate melted
3 ounces red chocolate melted
1 ounce black chocolate
Chocolate shoe mold

DIRECTIONS

Butter 8 -inch square pan. Melt chocolate and butter in 175 degrees oven for 10 minutes. Add vanilla, marshmallows and nuts. Stir until blended. Spread into pan and chill. Cut into squares before mixture gets too hard. Serve and enjoy!

For shoe, pour yellow chocolate into shoe mold leave sole of shoe without chocolate. Leave a small spot in the mold at the bottom of heel for black chhocolate. Place into freezer. When very cold , using red chocolate, place red chocolate on sole of shoe. Freeze. When very cold un mold shoe . Glue together with yellow chocolate. When ready to serve, place some cut rocky road in side. Enjoy!

PAIRS WELL WITH: Hot Chocolate and Godiva Liquer

White Chocolate Mousse Cake with Chocolate Lace

Serves 10 | Prep Time 1 hour | Cook Time 15 minutes

WHY I LOVE THIS RECIPE: A perfect dessert for company and for someone who loves chocolate but is allergic to dark chocolate. This cake is the lightest and most delicious. When purchasing your white chocolate for grating. Try to buy by the chunk. You want a good quality chocolate with a lot of cocoa butter added. The Belgium or Holland chocolates are my favorite. If desired , you could add raspberries , bananas or any fruit you desire to fill cake. I prefer just the white chocolate mousse.

INGREDIENTS YOU'LL NEED

White Chocolate Mousse:
12 ounces white chocolate, broken up
½ cup half and half
2 tablespoons softened sweet butter

2 cups heavy cream
* * *
Mousse Cake:
3 eggs, room temperature
1 egg yolk
½ cup sugar
½ teaspoon vanilla
½ cup flour
2 tablespoons butter, melted
* * *
Butter and flour for pan
* * *
1/8 cup Grand Marnier
6 ounces white chocolate, grated with potato peeler

DIRECTIONS

For White Chocolate Mousse place white chocolate and half and half in top of double boiler over hot water. Heat until chocolate melts. Cool mixture before adding cream. This can be done in microwave. Stir in butter until it melts. Remove from heat. Set aside. Add a little hot water and vanilla if chocolate becomes stiff. Whip cream until soft peaks form. Fold a little whipped cream into white chocolate to lighten. Fold in remaining whipped cream. Refrigerate until cake is ready to frost.

For Mousse Cake, combine 3 eggs, yolk, sugar, and vanilla in mixing bowl. Place bottom of bowl in boiling water a few seconds. Beat mixture on high for 6 minutes in an electric mixing bowl over high speed. Stir flour into the batter while folding in with spatula. Fold in butter the same way. For larger pieces of lace instead of grating white chocolate, chill a small marble board in the freezer wrapped in a towel overnight. With a spatula, spread quickly a small amount of chocolate across marble. , Lift quickly and reserve in the refrigerator on a saran wrap lined cookie sheet. Wrap cake in this once frosted.

Butter corners of 11" x 17" jelly roll pan. Place parchment paper in pan. Butter and flour parchment paper. Shake out excess flour. Pour mixture in pan and bake in preheated oven at 350 degrees for 15 minutes. Remove from oven and let stand 5 minutes. Place sheet of parchment paper on top of cake. Place cutting board over paper and turn cake upside down on it. Remove paper. Divide cake into 3 sections. Sprinkle cake with Grand Marnier. Cut through paper with knife to separate sections. Place 1 section on platter and spread with mousse. Place another cake layer on top and spread with mousse. Repeat for the last layer. Frost cake with mousse. Press white chocolate lace all over cake. Refrigerate until ready to serve. Enjoy!

you
ARE
your
HOME

Woven Chocolate Champagne Bucket

Serves Makes 6 small baskets | Prep Time 25 minutes | Cook Time No cooking time required

WHY I LOVE THIS RECIPE: This is a fun recipe to make and give each guest one to take home. this is something they will always remember. The food you make brings love into this world. That will heal everything. I learned to weave chocolate a long time ago when I was first married. There was a restaurant called Scandia and the Chef Henry invited me to come to the kitchen to learn how to make this. I will always remember his generous spirit and passion for food.

INGREDIENTS YOU'LL NEED

6 ounces semi-sweet chocolate bits
4 ounces white chocolate or white chocolate coating
2 ounces milk chocolate coating
a few drops green food coloring for chocolate

* * *

2 ounces Marzipan
gold dust
green chocolate for writing

DIRECTIONS

Melt chocolates in 3 separate bowls in 175 degrees oven for 30 minutes, stirring every 10 minutes. Fill wax paper cone tube with star tip, fitted in with semi-sweet chocolate. Using a small whiskey glass as a mold, take a piece of tin foil and firmly place all over glass. Working down first, pipe strips going in the opposite direction. Chill until very firm. Remove tin foil and refrigerate. Pipe rounds on wax paper for handles and chill. When firm, attach to both sides of bucket. Return to refrigerator. Chop white chocolate to be covering for ice cubes. chop marzipan into a small circle. Dip into chocolate. Chill on a Saran Wrap lined plate. Refrigerate and Reserve.

Mold marzipan into the shape of a champagne bottle. Melt white chocolate and mix in a little food color. Dip marzipan bottle completely into melted green chocolate, reserving the top. Chill on a plate lined with plastic wrap. Chill until shape is firm. Dip top in gold dust. Fill wax paper cone with small amount green chocolate. Pipe name of favorite champagne or persons initial in front of basket. Chill until ready to serve. Chill. Fill bucket with ice cubes and place champagne bottle in center. Glue in with white chocolate. Chill until ready to serve. Enjoy!

Poached Pears in Its Own Juices with Vanilla Bean

Serves 6 servings | Prep Time 10 minutes | Cook Time 40 minutes

WHY I LOVE THIS RECIPE: "Any fruit can actually be prepared this way. Apples and Peaches are especially good." This recipe is wonderful and truly easy to make. the results are delicious. You can even place a scoop of ice cream on top for an added adventure in eating. just enjoy!

INGREDIENTS YOU'LL NEED

6 ripe pears peeled and cored with stem left on
1 cup water
1 cup sparkling grape juice
1/4 cup honey
1 vanilla bean split

DIRECTIONS

Place all ingredients except pears in a large saucepan with lid. Mix thoroughly. place pears in liquid. Bring to a boil, then reduce heat and cover pan. Cook until pears are tender and liquid caramelizes. Enjoy!

PAIRS WELL WITH: Coffee or a cup of tea

The ocean and everything in it is a gift as we are to one another

Sauces, Stocks and Vinaigrettes

Sake Glaze

INGREDIENTS YOU'LL NEED

1/2 cup sake
1/2 cup rice wine vinegar
1 cup tamari
1/3 cup sesame oil
1/4 cup sweet onion
10 garlic cloves
1 tablespoon fresh ginger, peeled
1/3 cup cane sugar
1/4 cup honey

DIRECTIONS

Place all ingredients in a jar and shake well. refrigerate overnight to blend flavors. Enjoy.

Mustard Vinaigrette

INGREDIENTS YOU'LL NEED

1 Tbl. Dijon mustard
1 tsp. Colemans English Mustard
1 tsp. Worcesteshire sauce
1 Tbl. Egg white
1/2 Tbl. of organic cane sugar
1/2 Tsp. Himalayan pink salt
1/4 cup white Balsamic vinegar
1/2 cup Canola oil

DIRECTIONS

Combine all ingredients except oil i9n the work bowl of a food processor. With the motor running, gradually add the oil drop by drop through the feed tube until emulsified.

Remoulade Dressing

INGREDIENTS YOU'LL NEED

1 egg yolk
2 tablespoons agave nectar
1 teaspoon sea salt
¼ cup red wine vinegar
2 tablespoons tomato paste or catsup
1 tablespoon Dijon mustard
1 teaspoon dry mustard
1/4 cup water
1 teaspoon Worcestershire sauce
1 tablespoon sweet relish
2/3 cup canola oil
2 tablespoons Whipped cream, whipped

DIRECTIONS

Place all ingredients in work bowl of food processor, except oil and whipping cream.Slowly add oil through feed tube. Add whipping cream. Place in jar and refrigerate until needed. If desired, for every ½ cup dressing, stir in 2 tablespoons whipped cream. Follow instructions for recipe you are making.

Feta Vinaigrette

INGREDIENTS YOU'LL NEED

1 egg white
1 tablespoon Dijion musta3rd
2 tablespoons raw honey
1 tablespoon champagne vinegar
1 te4aspoon Worchestershire sauce
1/2 teaspoon sea salt
1/2 cup canola oil
1/4 cup Greek yogurt
1/4 cup feta cheese

DIRECTIONS

Combine all the ingredients to the work bowl of the food processor except, canola oil, yogurt and feta cheese. With motor running, gradually add the oil through the feed tube of the food processor. Add yogurt and cheese. Pulse for 10 seconds. Place in jar until ready to use.

Caesar Dressing

INGREDIENTS YOU'LL NEED

1 egg yolk
1 tablespoon English dry mustard
2 garlic cloves minced
1/4 cup anchovies
1 teaspoon Worcestershire sauce
Dash cayenne
1 tablespoon lemon juice
1/3 cup olive oil

DIRECTIONS

Place all ingredients of food processor and with the machine running, gradually add oil through the work bowl of the food processor. Place in jar and refrigerate

Red Wine Vinaigrette

INGREDIENTS YOU'LL NEED

1/4 cup red wine vinegar
1/4 cup fresh raspberries, for color
1 tablespoon dijion mustard
1/2 teaspoon dry Colemans English mustard
1 teaspoon Worcestershire sauce
2 tablespoons raw honey or cane sugar
1 teaspoon sea salt
2/3 cups canola oil

DIRECTIONS

Place all ingredients in the work bowl of the food processor and with the motor running , gradually add the oil through the feed tube. Strain to remove raspberry seeds and place in a jar. Refrigerate.

Homemade Mayonnaise

INGREDIENTS YOU'LL NEED

1 shallot chopped
1 clove fresh garlic minced
1 tablespoon olive oil
1 egg yolk
1 teaspoon sea salt
1/4 cup red wine vinegar
1 teaspoon Worcestershire sauce
1 tablespoon cane sugar
1 cup canola oil

DIRECTIONS

Heat olive oil in a small pan over very low heat. Add shallot and cook until translucent. stir in minced garlic and cook for a few moments. Place in the bowl of the food processor and when cool all all the other ingredients except oil. Gradually add the oil through the feed tube and refrigerate until needed.

Lemon Sauce

INGREDIENTS YOU'LL NEED

1 egg yolk
2 teaspoons honey
1 teaspoon dry English mustard
1 tablespoon lemon juice
1 teaspoon grated lemon peel
1 teaspoon Worcestershire sauce
1 teaspoon dijon mustard
1//2 cup canola oil
1/2 teaspoon himalayan salt

DIRECTIONS

Place all ingredients except oil in the work bowl of a food processor, gradually add oil with motor running through the feed tube.

Marinara Sauce

INGREDIENTS YOU'LL NEED

½ cup extra virgin olive oil
1 large onion, chopped
18 organic Roma tomatoes on the vine, chopped
5 garlic cloves, minced
2 tablespoons anchovies
½ teaspoon salt
1 tablespoon sugar
½ cup fresh basil
¼ cup fresh oregano

DIRECTIONS

Heat olive oil in large sauté pan. Add onions and sauté until lightly golden brown. Add tomatoes, garlic, anchovies, sea salt, and sugar and bring to boil. Reduce heat and simmer with basil and oregano. Simmer 30 to 40 minutes. Strain and set aside.

Tomato Sauce

INGREDIENTS YOU'LL NEED

10 roma tomatoes , very ripe and chopped
4 tablespoons extra virgin olive oil
1 sweet onion chopped
5 garlic cloves minced
2 cups, chicken broth
a sprig basil leaf
1 teaspoon sea salt
1 tablespoon cane sugar

DIRECTIONS

Heat olive oil in a 12-inch skillet. Add onions and cook until lightly golden brown, stir in garlic. Add tomatoes, basil leaf and salt. Cook for 3o minutes over low heat. Add chicken broth and sugar. Cook for 40 minutes over low heat. Cool and puree. Reserve.

Beet Glaze

INGREDIENTS YOU'LL NEED

½ cup beet juice
¼ cup maple syrup

DIRECTIONS

Mix together beet juice and maple syrup. Place in saucepan and reduce until thick.

Homemade Barbeque Sauce

INGREDIENTS YOU'LL NEED

4 cups catsup
1 cup yellow mustard
8 ounces currant jelly
1/3 cup natural liquid smoke or liquid smoke from your smoker
½ cup soy sauce
½ cup Worcestershire sauce
1½ cups pineapple juice
½ cup agave nectar or raw honey
½ cup brown sugar or 1/2 cup smoked brown sugar
1/2 cups molasses
2 teaspoons cocoa

DIRECTIONS

Combine all ingredients in large saucepan. Bring to boil. Reduce heat and simmer, stirring occasionally for 25 minutes. Store in jars in the refrigerator.

Dill Vinaigrette

INGREDIENTS YOU'LL NEED

¾ cup dill sprigs
½ cup chives
½ cup white wine vinegar
1½ tablespoons Dijon mustard
1 teaspoon dry mustard
1 tablespoon sugar
1 teaspoon Worcestershire sauce
1/3 teaspoon sea salt
¾ cup canola oil

DIRECTIONS

Place dill and chives in work bowl of food processor; add white wine vinegar. Process until very chopped and green. Add remaining ingredients, except oil. With the motor running, slowly add the canola oil until thick. Strain and set aside. Any left over dressing can be stored in refrigerator for several weeks and used for other salads.

Browned Beef Stock

INGREDIENTS YOU'LL NEED

5 short ribs
Sea salt to taste
1 teaspoon Dry mustard
¼ teaspoon Paprika
Dash Pepper
1 onion, chopped
3 carrots, chopped
3 celery stalks, chopped
5 whole garlic cloves
5 stalks thyme
1/3 cup extra virgin olive oil
10 cups water

DIRECTIONS

Season short ribs with salt, mustard, paprika, and pepper. Heat pan and sauté meat until brown on both sides. Brown the vegetables and place in pan with meat. Deglaze pan with water and pour over meat. Cover pan and bake at 475 degrees for 2 hours. Reduce heat to 200 degrees and bake 4 hours more. Cool in pan. Strain broth. Remove fat from broth and meat. Freeze broth and meat separately. May be prepared in advance and frozen.

Chicken Stock

INGREDIENTS YOU'LL NEED

5 backs and ribs from chicken, all skin and fat removed
3 carrots , peeled
3 celery ribs
1 red onion peeled
1/2 tablespoon kosher salt

DIRECTIONS

Place all ingredients in a large stock pot. Cover with water by 2 inches. Bring to boil, then lower heat and simmer for 3 to 4 hours. Skim fat as necessary. Strain and place in containers to freeze. Use as needed.

Vegetable Stock

INGREDIENTS YOU'LL NEED

5 carrots peeled
5 celery ribs
1 red onion
2 portabello onions
1 parsnip peeled
6 garlic cloves peeled
1/2 tablespoon kosher salt

DIRECTIONS

Place all ingredients in a large stockpot and cover with water and bring to a boil. Simmer for 3 hours.

Chili Vinaigrette

INGREDIENTS YOU'LL NEED

1/4 teaspoon chili sauce with garlic, available in Asian section in markets
2 tablespoons honey
1/4 teaspoon Himalayan salt
1 garlic clove, minced
1/4 teaspoon fresh grated ginger
1/2 tablespoon sesame oil
1 tablespoon rice wine vinegar

DIRECTIONS

Combine all ingredients.

White Garlic Beurre Blanc

1 shallot chopped
2 garlic cloves minced
4 tablespoon white wine vinegar
1/2 cup water
1 tablespoon fresh tarragon
1/2 teaspoon black peppercorns
1/2 stick unsalted butter cut in 6 pieces, cold
Pink salt to taste

In a small saucepan, combine all ingredients except butter. Bring to simmer. Cook over low heat until reduced to 2 tablespoon. Strain and discard garlic, shallots, peppercorns and tarragon. Place 2 tablespoons liquid in a small sauce pan.

When ready to serve, bring 2 tablespoons reserved liquid to simmer and gradually add cold butter 1/2 tablespoon at a time. Do not boil. If butter separates, add an ice cube and stir. Use as need. Season with pink salt.

Appendix

Lauren Lobley's Story

My husband, Ted McDonald, and I have resided in Malibu for almost a decade. Well, he had been in Malibu for much longer than that. I joined him in 2011after culinary school in Vancouver, Canada. I own and operate a yoga studio in the Malibu Country Mart called 5 Point Yoga. In February of 2016, we welcomed our first child, Madison Grace, into the world, and she happily took to life in Malibu.

The summer before the Woolsey Fire forced the mandatory evacuation of all Malibu residents, I had begun selling my vegan gluten free desserts at the Malibu Farmers Market. After getting requests from multiple, friends and strangers alike, I began a meal delivery service for the town of Malibu, offering up a new and fixed menu of vegan gluten free healthy savory and sweet food each week. The evening of November 8th, 2018, I was visiting a friend and her new baby in Agoura Hills. It was then that I experienced the smoke from the fire. The smoke was strong enough that it filled the air with a grey haze and I could hardly breathe. When I drove over Kanan that night on my way home to Point Dume, I had no idea that it would be the last time I would drive over Kanan in long time.

The morning of November 9th, around 7 a.m., we got our evacuation orders. My husband, daughter and I fled north to Ojai, to stay with some friends who- though they had a home in Malibu- were living there and running a golf course. I will never forget the fear in my heart as I drove toward Trancas along PCH, my daughter in her car seating's the back, and the car filled with the un mistakable smell of smoke. It was so thick. The light grew dark. At 8 a.m. it felt like 6 p.m. For 20 minutes, I gripped the steering wheel , nervously looking at the hills to my right(ocean to my left) , swearing that flames were going to envelope the everything, as I drove to Ojai. As we now know, they eventually did, but thankfully, not for many hours later, when my daughter and I (and my husband driving the other car behind me) were safe.

We got to Ojai at 10 a.m. where the sun was shining, the air was clear, the sky was blue and Malibu was a distant memory, safely behind us. My husband arrived soon after, and while we let our daughter to play with our friends daughter, our friends daughter is about the same age as ours), we adults were glued to the television, desperately hoping that the flames wouldn't reach our neighborhoods and Malibu would be spared.

By 5 p.m. that night , the friend's house where we fled to in Ojai learned that their primary residence in Malibu, had burned down. It was gut wrenching. It was so confusing to be present for someones grief when you yourself are in the midst of possibly experiencing that same reality. Because it wasn't over yet. The winds were still strong, and the fire was still spreading. With the roads closed and nowhere to go, we stayed and supported our friends and anxiously texted and called people who stayed in malibu to get word of our house. When the danger finally passed after a few days, and we learned that our home was still standing, we were relieved, but also devastated by the loss of so many of our friends homes, and so many of them not more than a mile from our house. We got lucky. A neighbor of ours stayed behind and was able to fend off the fires that would have ultimately taken our home(there was a fire burning on our front lawn). Will we ever be able to thank him? I think not. How do you thanks someone who saved you from the heartbreak of losing all your memories and experiences go up in flames? We tried. We said thank-you. But it fell flat. And so the only thing I can think to do is to pay it forward. To remember his actions and to promise I will spread that goodness out into the universe and come to the aid of those in need whenever we are able and capable.

The story could go on forever, but in the end, after being displaced for 2 1/2 months, and staying with some of the most amazing friends who took us in during that time, we ultimately decided to move out of Malibu. Our studio is still very much running in the Country mart, and we hope that it will be a safe haven for anyone who suffered any kind of loss or trauma from the Woolsey Fire. But as a family who has now welcomed our second child, Liam Edward, into the world in August of this year-a true fire baby, we made the decision to move out of the area amidst all of the clean up that m must inevitably happen.

Malibu will always have a special place in our hearts. As our friends rebuild, either in Malibu or elsewhere, we will always remember how fragile and precious life is, and how quickly everything can be taken away in an instant. I got into cooking and baking because of the way it brings people together, and even now- almost a year after the fires-we need to come together, to support each other. May this recipe be the base of many brunches and breakfasts with your friends and families, wherever you may reside. As you sit around the table, may your laughter and storytelling fill your homes-wherever you may be. May goodness and light follow you always. May we always remember that these moments are the one that make it all worth while.

MalibuStrong

Lisa McKean's Story

As avid sailors and newlyweds, we had just returned from our honeymoon sailing g for two weeks in the West Indies. We arrived home after a long and delayed journey at 4 a.m. Thursday morning. We fell asleep and awoke on November 9th and remember how silent everything was. An eerie foreboding silence. I turned my phone on and it started pinging and pinging, messages sent over the last few hours asking if we were okay, had we evacuated yet. I awakened Michael and said "I am not sure what is going on but I think there must be a fire near us!" Still calm, I stepped outside to see what else I could find out, and was hit by a strong scent of smoke. I walked out further on the deck and looked behind the house up at the mountains and there was swirling smoke blowing fast toward the coast. " Mike!" " Quick get up, there IS a fire and it seems to be heading our way!" Mike, having retired after 38 years with SMFD came out to have a look and was calm and re-assuring that he was sure the fire dept. would have things in hand. Meanwhile our neighbors appeared in their drive and said " We all need to evacuate now!:"

We had not even unpacked our suitcases from our honeymoon ocean voyage so we threw those in the car, loaded some of our wedding gifts, my photo albums and scrapbooks going back 50 years, important documents and for some reason a big down duvet and my feather pillows. That was it. Down to Zuma Beach where all the neighborhood had gathered along with skittish horses and lamas, anxious pets, wild animals and birds- all at the beach together. A strange calm and quiet enveloped us. A hush as we spoke to each other.

The fire grew more fierce and the towering mountain of smoke thousands of feet high, engulfed the coast and caught fire right down to PCH. We could see the flames marching straight into the heart of Malibu Park. At one point, Mike tried to drive back to our home but was caught in a howling fire on Phillip. With no vision , he blindly spun the car around and escaped, I was so grateful to see his face re-appear and standing there hugging him at the side of PCH.

The smoke became too much for everyone at Zuma so we all headed for Westward beach and stood in front of the Sunset.

The fire was now advancing and had jumped the coast highway heading into Point Dume. We needed to get away again and so drove back to Zuma.

At around 3 o'clock, just six hours after we had awakened so unaware of how lives would change in that short time, we decided to head t Ventura. As we passed Guernsey, I motioned from my car to Mike in his, let's first go back and see if our home survived. We turned right and on up to Harvester. As we rounded the corner to Harvester, total desolation appeared before before before our eyes, smoky ruins dotted the rolling hills now covered in black and grew ash. All of our good neighbor's homes were totally destroyed. Then we came upon ours and it was in flames. We jumped out of our cars at the bottom of the drive and could see half the house burning and our bedroom, where we had so gratefully rested our heads after thousands of miles of sailing, on the brink of destruction. I so wanted to rush to it and have one last chance to grab some precious belongings. It was too late. Michael had only just finished building our home a year before. We were in shock. Married in may, burnt out in November, we drove away with tears in our eyes.

Melanie Goudzwaard's Story

We lost our home of 20 years on November 9, when the Woolsey Fire roared through our canyon near Westward Beach and we saw the house burn in front of us. Like so many others, we were displaced for weeks and had to find a new place to live while we began to process and grieve for our home and former lives. It has been a hard few months, going through our daughter's senior year at high school and the college admissions process, and trying to find a new normal. We are trying to rebuild our home but are still some months away from a building permit, and it's hard to know what the future really holds and where we will be living in a few years time. We have been sustained by the incredible outpouring of support and kindness from the local community and from friends far and wide, and we take comfort knowing we are not alone and many of our friends are walking the same path with us.

I lost dozens of cookery books in the fire along with everything else we owned, and many handed down recipes that I can't get again. When I was asked to contribute to this book I chose a recipe from my childhood back in the UK, and one I know from heart, and didn't have to source online—Shepherd's Pie. It was one of the first things I made for my family when we finally had a place to call "home" again and were no longer camping with friends. It's a hearty dish, real comfort food, and something my American family and friends always appreciate. I hope to make this again in my own, rebuilt home one day.

Meet the Design Team

Cathy Rogers, author and recipe creator

Gina Burrell, editor

Annie Gingold, photographer

Recipe Index